✯✯✯✯✯✯✯✯✯✯✯✯✯✯✯✯✯

BASEBALL SUPERSTARS

Babe Ruth

✯✯✯✯✯✯✯✯✯✯✯✯✯✯✯✯✯

Hank Aaron
Ty Cobb
Johnny Damon
Lou Gehrig
Rickey Henderson
Derek Jeter
Randy Johnson
Andruw Jones
Mickey Mantle
Roger Maris

Mike Piazza
Kirby Puckett
Albert Pujols
Mariano Rivera
Jackie Robinson
Babe Ruth
Curt Schilling
Ichiro Suzuki
Bernie Williams
Ted Williams

BASEBALL SUPERSTARS

Babe Ruth

Tracy Brown Collins

CHELSEA HOUSE
PUBLISHERS

An imprint of Infobase Publishing

BABE RUTH

Chelsea House
An imprint of Infobase Publishing
132 West 31st Street
New York NY 10001

Library of Congress Cataloging-in-Publication Data
Collins, Tracy Brown, 1972-
  Babe Ruth / Tracy Brown Collins.
    p. cm. — (Baseball superstars)
  Includes bibliographical references and index.
  ISBN 978-0-7910-9570-6 (hardcover)
  1. Ruth, Babe, 1895-1948. 2. Baseball players—United States—Biography. I. Title.
II. Series.
  GV865.R8C65 2008
  796.357092—dc22
  [B]   2007028935

Chelsea House books are available at special discounts when purchased in bulk quantities for businesses, associations, institutions, or sales promotions. Please call our Special Sales Department in New York at (212) 967-8800 or (800) 322-8755.

You can find Chelsea House on the World Wide Web at http://www.chelseahouse.com

Series design by Erik Lindstrom
Cover design by Ben Peterson

Printed in the United States of America

Bang EJB 10 9 8 7 6 5 4 3 2 1

This book is printed on acid-free paper.

All links and Web addresses were checked and verified to be correct at the time of publication. Because of the dynamic nature of the Web, some addresses and links may have changed since publication and may no longer be valid.

CONTENTS

George Ruth's Rough Start

On the brink of the twentieth century, baseball was still quite young. Legend has it that the game was invented by a man called Abner Doubleday in Cooperstown, New York. Doubleday was credited with naming baseball and creating its rules, although no proof has ever existed to back the story. In reality, the game that would become America's pastime evolved over time from similar games like cricket and rounders, which had their origins in the United Kingdom. In 1845, Alexander Joy Cartwright drafted the first published rules of the game, and in 1867, a player by the name of Candy Cummings threw baseball's very first curveball.

The game continued to evolve. In 1876, baseball's National League was founded, with teams like the Boston Red Stockings, the Hartford Dark Blues, and Mutual of New York. (The league was followed a quarter of a century later by the American League, which included teams like the Chicago White Stockings, the Milwaukee Brewers, and the Detroit Tigers. In 1903, the winning teams from both leagues faced each other in the first World Series.) As the turn of the century approached, one of baseball's biggest stars was Cy Young. His extraordinary pitching amazed fans, and to this day the Cy Young Award is given annually to the best pitcher in each league.

Also around this time, another player who left a definite mark on the game was born. This player not only became one of baseball's highest-paid and biggest stars but also permanently altered the strategy of the game. His celebrity and personality drew people to the sport as he pounded out home run after home run—714 in all, a record that would stand for almost 40 years.

TOUGH EARLY YEARS

That player, George Herman Ruth, was born on February 6, 1895, in Baltimore, Maryland. For much of his life, George Ruth would believe he was born on February 7, 1894. He learned about the mistake in 1934 when he was required to show his birth certificate in order to get a passport. When Ruth got his birth certificate from Baltimore, it showed the 1895 birth date. He was born at his grandmother's home, just a block from where Oriole Park at Camden Yards stands. Coincidentally, the house in which Ruth's parents lived at the time stood right where Oriole Park's center field is today. The neighborhood in which Ruth was born was known as Pigtown—so named because of the hundreds of pigs that would run through it on their way to the local slaughterhouse. People who lived there are said to have grabbed pigs off the streets for their Sunday dinners. The neighborhood was poor and rough, full of cramped houses near the docks.

Ruth's parents, Kate and George, Sr., owned and ran a bar, and their home was upstairs from their business. They had

The house where Babe Ruth was born in 1895 *(above)* is now the center-piece of the Babe Ruth Birthplace and Museum in Baltimore, Maryland. Ruth was born at his grandmother's house, which is only a block from Oriole Park at Camden Yards. The home in which Ruth's parents lived at the time stood where center field at Oriole Park is today.

eight children, yet only George Herman and his sister Mary survived past infancy. His early years are a bit of a mystery. As an adult, Ruth did not talk much about his childhood. We know he was a rebellious child who was frequently in trouble: skipping school, getting into fights, drinking, committing petty crimes. In Ruth's memoir, *Babe Ruth's Own Book of Baseball,* he describes his childhood surroundings:

> My earliest recollections center about the dirty, traffic-crowded streets of Baltimore's riverfront.

Crowded streets they were, too, noisy with the roar of heavy trucks whose drivers cursed and swore and aimed blows with their driving whips at the legs of kids who made the streets their playground.

And the youngsters, running wild, struck back and echoed the curses. Truck drivers were our enemies: So were the coppers patrolling their beats, and so too were the shopkeepers who took bruising payment from our skins for the apples and the fruit we "snitched" from their stands and counters.

A rough, tough neighborhood, but I liked it.

Ruth recalls that many people in his neighborhood thought that he was an orphan, presumably because he spent so much time running the streets in dirty clothes and because he frequently had little to eat. Not much is known about Ruth's parents. His father is painted as a temperamental man who was good at business and ran many taverns throughout his life. Ruth's mother is an even bigger mystery. Only one known photo of her exists—a family portrait in which she holds Ruth on her lap. She would have been pregnant most of her adult years until her death at 39 of, according to her death certificate, "exhaustion." Her identity is clouded in conflicting information. Her death certificate claims she was a widow, which was wrong. Ruth would claim his mother was Irish and English, while his sister said she was German.

THE TROLLEY TO ST. MARY'S

What is known is that Ruth's parents must have figured out that they could no longer control their son, and so they sent him to a school for troubled boys. In his autobiography, *The Babe Ruth Story*, which was ghostwritten for him just before his death, Ruth says of his childhood, "I had a rotten start, and it took me a long time to get my bearings." The school where he was sent, called St. Mary's Industrial School for Boys, was the first important step in finding his bearings.

On June 13, 1902, young George boarded the Wilkens Avenue trolley with his father and headed for his new life at St. Mary's. Ruth never really talked about this day, so we can only guess the mood. In the opening of his biography *The Big Bam*, former *Boston Globe* sports columnist Leigh Montville tries to recreate the scene:

> The man is sad or resolute or perhaps secretly happy. The boy is . . . does he even know where he is going? Is the packed little suitcase on the seat next to him a clue? Or is there no suitcase? He is dressed in the best clothes that he owns. Or are there no best clothes? The conversation is quiet, short sentences, the man's mind lost somewhere in the business of the moment. Or perhaps there is no conversation, not a word. Or perhaps there are laughs, the man talking and talking, joking, to take the edge away.

Life at St. Mary's would have been a significant change for George, who was used to coming and going as he pleased and not obeying any rules. The Xaverian Brothers, a Catholic religious order, ran the school. When he arrived there, the school had about 800 boys in residence—half of them sent there by local and state courts. Life was very disciplined. The boys went to bed at 8:00 P.M. sharp and awoke at 6:00 A.M. sharp. The school had opened in 1866, in response to the growing number of children who were left orphans during the Civil War. The increase in orphans was the state's burden, and the quality of life in the overcrowded orphanage system declined. The Reverend Martin Spaulding, the archbishop of Baltimore at the time, opened St. Mary's to provide an alternative to the state orphanages. He feared that Catholic orphans would otherwise lose their religion. For this reason, as with other Catholic orphanages, children who were brought to St. Mary's tended to stay there rather than be adopted by other families, who might not have been Catholic. George was in and out of the school from 1902 to 1904, staying for about a month the first two times. Finally, in 1904, St. Mary's became his home. He stayed there for four years before leaving in 1908. Two years later, after his mother died, George returned to St. Mary's.

LIFE IN A BOARDING SCHOOL

In his book *Building the Invisible Orphanage: A Prehistory of the American Welfare System*, Matthew A. Crenson describes the conditions in Catholic orphanages and live-in schools like St. Mary's as far from perfect. "A lot of orphanages featured marching drills," Crenson writes, "like those you'd see in those old-fashioned prison movies. Most of them had corporal punishment, usually with leather straps. Solitary confinement up to a week was the punishment for some offenses." The food was rotten, and the boys were forced to work very hard.

The kids at the school all had nicknames, unflattering names assigned by the other boys. Seven-year-old George Ruth was no exception. His nickname was a racial slur that made reference to his lips and nose, which were considered to resemble those of the day's African-American stereotype. Ruth was often "accused" of having African-American bloodlines owing to his facial features, although this claim does not seem to have any basis. Ruth's nickname—which he hated—would stay with him for most of his years at St. Mary's. Ruth, though, was a big and temperamental kid, and for these reasons, the other boys mostly left him alone.

Although the school was a Catholic institution, religious training was not a primary focus. Schoolwork was actually not the main focus, either: Discipline was. One of the Xaverian Brothers—a brother being more like a male nun than a priest—would teach academics, and the rest would teach a skill that would, it was hoped, lead to a job for the children later, such as shoemaking, woodworking, gardening, or farming. George excelled the most in the tailor shop, where he sewed shirts, and he eventually became so good that he landed a job in what was called the High City Tailor Shop. The best clothes were made at the shop, which was in the school's laundry building. Although the practice was later prohibited, the boys who worked in the tailor shop were able to earn money working on shirts for the local Oppenheim Shirt Company. Ruth and the other boys made about six cents per shirt.

Later as a major-league ballplayer, fans adored Ruth for his generosity with his time and money. He created numerous charities, particularly for children. He gave money to help fund business ventures of his former St. Mary's classmates. This generosity was evident even in his days at St. Mary's. Ruth frequently took the money that he made working as a tailor and used it to buy candy for the younger boys at the school. Ruth also used to walk around the recess yard during the cold winter months, going from boy to boy, rubbing their arms and blowing on their hands to try to keep them warm. This concern and attention earned him favor and popularity with the younger students. Baseball turned him into a school star.

GEORGE PLAYS BALL

Although life was not always ideal in the school, one of the Xaverian Brothers who was in charge of keeping the boys in line became one of Babe Ruth's biggest heroes. On more than one occasion, Ruth would say he was the greatest man he ever knew. His name was Brother Matthias. During recreation time, Brother Matthias used to hit what were called "fungoes" to the boys in a field—a "fungo" was when you hit a long pop fly by tossing the ball in the air with one hand and then swinging the bat.

In *The Big Bam*, Brother Thomas More Page, who had been a resident at St. Mary's, remembers the experience:

> What I think every boy who was at St. Mary's at the time will remember are the Saturday evenings after supper whenever the news got around that Brother Matthias would

be hitting baseballs. Then, every boy in the school from all the five yards would gather in the upper yard, over 500 of us, awaiting the occasion. He would stand at the bottom of the steps and, with what seemed like an effortless motion, hit a ball with a fungo bat in his right hand only, while up and up the ball seemed to soar, almost out of sight, and then when it came down there was a mad scramble for it. We knew the end was coming to this extraordinary exhibition when he hit one ball after the other in rapid succession, and the balls kept falling down like snowflakes over the entire yard.

As a young boy, George watched in awe along with the other boys as Brother Matthias hit the ball far and long. Ruth said he knew then that he was born to be a hitter. Brother Matthias worked hard with George and taught him how to field and throw a ball. With Matthias's help, George discovered something he loved that he was good at. Spending so much time with Brother Matthias gave him credibility with the other boys, all of whom admired Matthias, and life for George became easier at St. Mary's.

THE BASEBALL OBSESSION

Baseball was a very big deal at St. Mary's. The school offered a variety of sports for the boys—football, basketball, soccer, wrestling—but baseball was an obsession at the school as well as across the nation. There were three times as many baseball teams at St. Mary's as basketball teams. In 1909, 28 teams existed at the school. Babe Ruth later said that he played about 200 games a year during his time at the school, up to two or three a day. As the sport became more and more popular, Brother Matthias and others formed a league made up of the oldest and best players at St. Mary's. The teams in the league were named after actual teams of the day: the Cubs, the White Sox, and the Giants, for example.

A young Babe Ruth *(right)* conferred with a teammate during a game in 1912. Although Ruth entered the major leagues as a pitcher, he often played catcher while at St. Mary's Industrial School for Boys. He enjoyed being the catcher because he could be involved in every play.

George played for the Red Sox. He was a large kid and was rather tough, which made him an excellent catcher. George was left-handed, but he had to play with a right-handed glove. He would wear the glove on his left hand, his throwing hand, to catch the ball, then tuck the glove behind his right arm, grab the ball with his left hand, and throw it. George played other positions, too, but he liked being the catcher because he could be involved in every play. It is said that during one game, his team was losing badly, and he was making fun of the pitcher. As a lesson, Brother Matthias told George that he should try pitching. George surprised Matthias and his team by shutting the other team down—he pitched a perfect game during which the other team got no hits.

George became the baseball star of St. Mary's. Baseball truly became his life. He played as often as he could, playing more, some said, than the average professional baseball player. During the summer months, George was given permission to play for amateur teams in the community outside of the school. Local newspapers ran stories of a pitcher named "Roth" who had great success on the mound.

RUTH MEETS JACK DUNN

The Xaverian Brothers also ran a college, Mount St. Joseph's, in Baltimore. Mount St. Joseph's had a baseball team, and the brothers could be fiercely competitive about their teams. In 1913, Brother Gilbert, the baseball coach at Mount St. Joseph's, was bragging about his best pitcher, Bill Morrisette. In turn, the brothers of St. Mary's began to brag about George Ruth. In the end, it was decided that a game would be played between St. Mary's and Mount St. Joseph's, which would really be more of a match between Ruth and Morrisette.

Jack Dunn was the owner and manager of the Baltimore Orioles, a minor-league team. He was also a scout of sorts—back then, the owners of minor-league clubs could sell players to the major-league teams. So Dunn was always on the lookout for new talent. Dunn had heard of Morrisette and planned to attend the game to see if he was good enough to sign a contract with the Orioles (which he did do later on).

The boys of St. Mary's were very excited about the game. They looked at Mount St. Joseph's as a snobby place full of boys they wanted to beat. Everyone looked forward to the game. Then, the word spread that George Ruth had run away from the school. Because he was the team's key player, the news brought the school to a standstill. Classes were canceled. Neighborhoods in Baltimore were searched. Eventually, Ruth returned and was punished by being forced to stand on a road during recess time for five straight days. At that point, Brother Matthias handed Ruth his glove and told him to start to practice for the game.

St. Mary's did more than beat the Mount St. Joseph's team. Led by Ruth on the mound, St. Mary's shut its opponents out. The final score was 6-0. Ruth struck out 22 players in the game and caught Dunn's eye.

★ ★ ★ ★ ★ ★

JACK DUNN

Jack Dunn was born in Meadville, Pennsylvania, in 1872. When Jack was just nine years old, his arm was run over by a boxcar while he played on the railroad tracks with some other kids. The doctor said he would have to lose the arm or risk death, but Jack insisted that he keep his arm. The boy wanted to be a baseball player, and he would rather have died than give up his arm. Jack survived without the surgery, and even though his damaged arm limited his skills, he did make the major leagues. Dunn played various positions during his eight-year career in the major leagues, including pitching for Brooklyn.

In 1907, Dunn became the manager of the Baltimore Orioles, a minor-league team that has no connection to today's major-league club. The following year, he bought the team. With his eye for recruiting, Dunn was able to build the club into a successful one, armed with the best new talent—including George Ruth in 1914. Another player whom Dunn signed was Lefty Grove, a Hall of Fame pitcher with the Philadelphia Athletics and the Boston Red Sox. Dunn's Orioles won seven straight International League titles from 1918 to 1924. Dunn ran the Orioles until his death in 1928 of a heart attack.

Jack Dunn, the man who signed Babe Ruth to his first professional base-ball contract, played for several major-league teams, including the New York Giants. Here, he was in action during a 1902 game at the Polo Grounds in New York. Dunn achieved much success as the owner of the minor-league Baltimore Orioles.

RUTH SIGNS A CONTRACT

There are differing accounts of how Dunn came to offer Ruth a contract. Initially, Brother Gilbert was credited with persuading Dunn to take a chance on Ruth. The brothers of St. Mary's had other versions of the story, all of which made Gilbert out to be a villain. One such story is that Gilbert was afraid that Dunn would offer a contract to Morrisette and that he would lose his star pitcher. Another is that Gilbert was angry with the brothers of St. Mary's for not allowing him to "borrow" Ruth for an important game, and so he led Dunn to Ruth out of spite.

Whatever the case, in February 1914, Dunn appeared at St. Mary's, sat down with Ruth and the school's superintendent, and offered Ruth a deal. The contract would be for $600 for one season with the Baltimore Orioles. That was $100 a month for six months. This was not a huge sum, really, but to Ruth it was all the money in the world and a chance to do what he loved. According to *The Babe Ruth Story*, Ruth reacted like this: "I guess I must have come near falling over in my excitement. Did I want to play baseball? Does a fish like to swim or a squirrel climb trees? I didn't even pause to ask questions. 'Sure,' I said. 'I'll play. When do I start?'" And so, two weeks later on February 27, Ruth left St. Mary's for good, as a professional baseball player.

Ruth
Gets His Shot

George Ruth left St. Mary's on February 27, 1914, a Friday. He had three days before the Orioles were to leave for spring training in Fayetteville, North Carolina. Ruth spent the weekend with his father, still the manager of a bar in Baltimore. It is hard to imagine what must have been going through Ruth's mind. He had never been on a train. Never been out of Baltimore. Now he was about to start a new life—one he had likely never thought to imagine.

Coming from the heavily disciplined setting of St. Mary's, where physical activity was greatly encouraged, Ruth was in prime condition at 6-foot-2 (188 centimeters) and 180 pounds (82 kilograms). The potbellied figure of his legend was not yet realized. The team he had signed with was mostly made up of older players. Five of the eight starters were over 30; one was 28. They were all veterans of the major leagues. Ruth's physical condition and youth were assets, but they did not overwhelm the experience and maturity of his teammates. He was not an immediate star. He had a lot to learn about the world he had just entered.

SPRING TRAINING

Come Monday morning, Ruth made his way through a Baltimore that had been devastated by a weekend blizzard. He was to meet up with Orioles owner/manager Jack Dunn—his new boss—at the Kernan Hotel. Twelve players were there, ready to head to Fayetteville; the storm had delayed other team members from getting to Baltimore. Ten of the 12 players were pitchers, like Ruth. Among them was Bill Morrisette, his rival from Mount St. Joseph's. The team headed for Union Station, not expecting the train to leave on time because of the storm, but the train was not delayed and the journey was uneventful. For Ruth, though, it had to be a great adventure, riding a train for the first time, wearing a new suit with money in his pockets.

His teammates wasted no time in finding ways to tease the 19-year-old Ruth. The other players told Ruth that the mesh hammock next to his bed in the train cabin was a device for pitchers to rest their arms in while they slept (it was actually a place to store clothing). Ruth spent the night with his arm uncomfortably held in the hammock, resulting in a stiff and sore arm the next morning.

In Fayetteville, Ruth was no less in awe of everything. He was more out of his element than he had ever been. The elevator in the Hotel Lafayette, where the team stayed, amazed him. He rose every morning at 5 A.M., a habit from his days at St. Mary's but not one he would keep forever. The weather was cold and wet in Fayetteville. The players tried to practice on the field, but it was full of puddles. As it continued to rain throughout the week, coach Scout Steinmann arranged with the mayor

Before joining the Baltimore Orioles of the International League, catcher Ben Egan played for the Philadelphia Athletics of the American League in 1908 and 1912. At Baltimore, he caught for a new pitcher, Babe Ruth. "It would be pleasant to say that I developed Ruth as a pitcher, but that would be hogwash," Egan later said. "He knew how to pitch the first day I saw him."

for the team to practice in the armory, a building only large enough to accommodate little more than a game of catch. The team settled for games of handball and even a basketball game against a local high school team.

Ruth's teammates largely ignored him during spring training. He was not only younger than most of the men, but he was also totally unsophisticated. Many of the men on the team were college-educated and worldly by comparison. His wonder at simple things, like the hotel elevator, which he continued to ride up and down for pleasure, amused his teammates but also demonstrated how little in common they had with him. The players did not talk with him much and did little to counsel him on the field, but fortunately for Ruth, he did not need much grooming.

The Orioles' star catcher, Ben Egan, said much later in life that "it would be pleasant to say that I developed Ruth as a pitcher, but that would be hogwash. He knew how to pitch the first day I saw him. I didn't have to tell him anything. He knew how to hold runners on base, and he knew how to work on the hitters. He was a pretty good pitcher on his own."

Finally on Saturday—five days after the team's arrival in North Carolina—the rain let up. The team was split into two squads for a seven-inning scrimmage. Nearly 200 locals showed up at the Fair Grounds to watch the game. Ruth was put in at shortstop. In the second inning, he had his first professional at-bat. What happened next made a big impression on everyone who watched. Ruth hit the ball deep into right field, farther than anyone who witnessed it had ever seen. Rodger Pippen of the *Baltimore News-American* summed it up like this: "The next batter made a hit that will live in the memory of all who saw it. That clouter was George Ruth, the southpaw from St. Mary's school. The ball carried so far to right field that he walked around the bases." Coincidentally, it was Bill Morrisette who was playing in the outfield and had to chase down Ruth's ball.

Later in the game, Ruth had the chance to pitch, which he did skillfully. The newspapers claimed, "This boy is the prize beauty of the rookies in the camp." Still, his home run was what made the lasting impression.

GEORGE BECOMES "BABE"

Throughout his career, George Ruth would have many nicknames. Among them, "The Sultan of Swat," "The Bambino,"

"The Colossus of Clout," "The Wali of Wallop," "The Wazir of Wham," "The Maharajah of Mash," "The Rajah of Rap," "The Caliph of Clout," "The Big Bam," and "The Behemoth of Bust." But George Ruth received his first and most lasting nickname soon after he came to the attention of sportswriters.

As with many things to do with Ruth, there are several versions of how the nickname "Babe" came to be. The most

☆ ☆ ☆ ☆ ☆
HOW SPORTSWRITERS MADE LEGENDS

The popularity of sportswriters—journalists who covered sports and the teams and athletes that played them—rose steeply from 1915 to 1925, when the newspaper pages dedicated to sports all over the country doubled. This demand not only served the professional sports industry well, but it also helped create legends of athletes like Babe Ruth.

Sportswriters had intimate relationships with the athletes they covered. They traveled with the teams and hung out with the players, chatting casually on the bench during a game or practice or rubbing shoulders with them at a bar. Rather than threaten their objectivity, sportswriters argued that this level of closeness allowed them the best access to players on and off the field, which gave them plenty of rich material to report. The writers, like all columnists, sought popularity in their readership, and they were more credible when they were up close to the heroes and icons of the day. Many celebrities today would hesitate to expose themselves so completely to the media, but times were different then. People wanted to read about the heroics of those they looked up to rather than focus on their faults or misfortunes.

Sportswriter Paul Gallico said of the relationship between writer and subject, "We sing of their muscles, their courage, common and probably the most accurate is that Oriole coach Steinmann had asked the team members to go easy on the rookie, because he was one of "Dunnie's Babes"—a favorite of the manager's. "Babe" was not an uncommon nickname of the day, but Babe Ruth soon became *the* Babe.

According to Ruth's autobiography, his success during spring training was not a surprise. "I went with the Orioles

☆ ☆ ☆ ☆ ☆

their gameness and skill because it seems to amuse readers and sells papers, but we rarely consider them as people and strictly speaking, leave their characters alone because that is dangerous ground." Indeed, Babe Ruth's behavior off the field was not reported on as it surely would be today. Instead, writers focused on his incredible abilities on the field and helped build his legend even for those who would never see him play live.

The writing style, too, was different from today—because it was a writer's job to bring to life mythic characters of the sports arena to an audience that had no other access to the athletes. Columns were written in a poetic style, laden with metaphor, rather than a more direct style that merely reported the facts.

For example, as cited in Leigh Montville's *The Big Bam*, Damon Runyon, then a columnist for the *New York American*, wrote this about Ruth: "No man has ever lived who hit a baseball as hard as Ruth. In the olden days, soldiers were equipped with slings and slew their enemies with missiles thrown from these slings, but it is doubtful if they got as much force behind them as Ruth puts back of a batted ball. The weapon which was the nearest approach to Babe's deadly drive was the catapult."

and was fortunate enough to make good," the book says. "In fact, I never for a moment thought that I wouldn't. I don't believe I was cocky, and I don't believe I was any fresher than the average rookie who gets a chance to sign a contract—but I was confident."

Perhaps more than confident, the rebellious trickster from his early days on the streets of Baltimore began to rear his head once the Babe was away from St. Mary's. He gambled. He got into other trouble, too. In his book *The Big Bam*, Leigh Montville shares two stories of Ruth's taste for adventure. One story is that of Ruth wanting to learn to ride a horse. The stable owner put Ruth on a Shetland pony for his first lesson, a pony that Ruth rode into an ice-cream shop, a pony that he tried to buy an ice cream for before being thrown out by an unamused shop owner who said he did not serve ponies.

Another story tells of Ruth borrowing a bicycle from a local kid and riding it into a hay wagon, a stunt that Jack Dunn witnessed. Dunn gave Ruth a harsh warning, shouting, "You wanna go back to that school? You behave yourself, you hear me? You're a ballplayer, not a circus act." Ruth's raw talent continued to keep him in solid favor with Dunn, who, for all of Ruth's antics, adored the kid. Dunn wrote to Brother Gilbert of Mount St. Joseph's College, saying, "Brother, this fellow Ruth is the greatest young ballplayer who ever reported to a training camp." To writers, he quietly said, "He'll startle the baseball world if he isn't a rummy or he isn't a nut."

THE BABE RETURNS TO BALTIMORE

When spring training was over, Ruth and the Orioles returned to Baltimore for the official start of the season. The Babe bought himself a motorcycle with his earnings. He did not ride well—as in other areas of his life, he rode recklessly, crashing several times before arriving back on the campus of St. Mary's to show off a little.

The Orioles were part of the International League, a minor league that still exists today, although it has gone through many changes since it began in 1884. Originally, all professional teams played in one league, but that soon became unmanageable. Eight of the best and richest teams broke away to form the National League in 1876, leaving the remaining teams to form their own organizations as minor-league teams.

The International League was formed as a merger of three other leagues, the Eastern League, the New York State League, and the Ontario League. In 1904, the league was running strong. People everywhere flocked to baseball games, creating a demand for new stadiums and, of course, creating a lucrative business for team owners. In 1914, however, the league took a hit when a new major league, the Federal League, formed. This was bad news for Jack Dunn, especially because the new league chose Baltimore as one of its home cities.

A TOUGH DECISION FOR JACK DUNN

Baltimore's new major-league team, the Terrapins, won over the people of the city. Baltimore had lost its own major-league team in 1903, when it moved to New York (eventually to become the Yankees), and people were thrilled to see their city once again join the major leagues. Although organized baseball did not recognize the new league as legitimate, the new Baltimore team was able to take players from other major-league ball clubs, which excited the fans. A new stadium was built across the street from where the Orioles played. Jack Dunn had a great team and a star rookie on his hands, but he was losing money. It is estimated that only 5,000 people total saw Ruth play his first year, while across the street nearly six times as many cheered on the Terrapins each game.

Dunn made several attempts to save his club. One attempt was to organize a series of three exhibition games against the major-league New York Giants, a team that had won the National League pennant three times in a row. The Orioles managed a victory in the first game, and it was during that game that Ruth first won the notice of the fans. Excited by the victory, he tossed the ball into the crowd, which the fans loved.

Ruth had good days and bad days. He hit well but did not match his home-run performance from Fayetteville. He was still learning. In the third exhibition game against the Giants, Ruth was pitching, and a miscommunication between Ruth

☆ ☆ ☆ ☆ ☆

THE FEDERAL LEAGUE

The Federal League existed for three seasons—from 1913 to 1915—and in its last two seasons, it aimed to operate as a major league, challenging the National League and the American League.

When it formed in the spring of 1913, the Federal League was an independent league but did not have plans to raid the major leagues for players. The strategy for many teams was to hire a well-known manager and then stock the clubs with experienced free-agent players and promising youngsters. Franchises were placed in Chicago, Pittsburgh, Cleveland, St. Louis, Indianapolis, and Cincinnati. Each of those cities except Indianapolis already had major-league teams. The first pennant winner in that debut season was Indianapolis, which finished with a 75–45 record, 10 games ahead of second-place Cleveland.

In 1914, the Federal League declared that it was a major league, and it expanded into Buffalo, Brooklyn, and Baltimore (where it challenged Jack Dunn's International League team). Also before that season, the Cleveland club had disbanded and the Cincinnati team had relocated to Kansas City. The Federal League now had clubs in four cities with major-league teams. In fact, St. Louis and Chicago each had three major-league teams. Indianapolis again won the title, but by only 1½ games over Chicago.

and Egan, the catcher, occurred that has become part of the Babe Ruth legend.

The Orioles were ahead, 2-1, in the ninth inning. The Giants had a runner on first. Egan gave Ruth the sign—a

☆ ☆ ☆ ☆ ☆ ☆

Officially, the Federal League was still respecting major-league contracts. But teams in the American League and the National League began to play tough after having contract disputes with players who pitted the leagues against each other. The Federal League enticed some major-league stars, and the major leagues and the upstart Feds filed lawsuits back and forth.

The 1915 season was one of the closest of any league. Six of the eight teams were in the pennant race until the last week. The championship was not decided until the final day of the season when Chicago and Pittsburgh split a doubleheader. Chicago finished at 86–66, just ahead of St. Louis (87–67) and Pittsburgh (86–67). Still, even with the nail-biting title race, attendance was lackluster and several teams needed financial assistance from the league to finish the season.

In December 1915, an agreement was reached between the Federal League and the major leagues. The Federal League was disbanded, and owners of the teams were compensated in various ways. Some owners were allowed to buy existing major-league teams. So ended the Federal League after three seasons—the last notable attempt to start a third major league in baseball.

RUTH
PITCHER
INTERNATIONAL
LEAGUE   BALTO.

This 1914 baseball card shows Babe Ruth when he was a player for Baltimore of the International League. While he was with the Orioles, Ruth acquired the "Babe" nickname. As the season progressed, team owner Jack Dunn was impressed with Ruth's play and eventually tripled his salary.

clenched fist—for a "waste" pitch, which is a pitch that is high and outside the strike zone in order to make it difficult to hit. Egan was trying to prevent a "hit and run," a play in which the base runners begin to advance before the ball is hit. Ruth interpreted the signal as a "waist" pitch, which he took to mean a pitch waist-high. He delivered the pitch, and the batter hit a two-run homer, winning the game. Both the catcher and the pitcher were furious, and both blamed the other for the famous miscommunication.

A rookie mistake. But once the season began, Ruth pitched shutouts and hit well when he made contact with the ball. A month after joining the team, Dunn doubled the amount of Ruth's contract. A month later, he added another $600, tripling the original amount to $1,800 a year. In July 1914, Dunn's Orioles were in first place in the International League, but nobody in Baltimore really cared. In his autobiography, Ruth said the manager of the Terrapins approached him to play for his team. Ruth turned down the offer because he had heard that players who switched to the Federal League would be banned from baseball for life. A Terrapin official at the time claimed that what Ruth said was not true, that they had agreed not to approach any of Dunn's players.

The Orioles continued to play well to smaller and smaller crowds. Dunn, a businessman, knew when to call it quits. He talked with a group of men from Virginia who offered him $62,500 to own 49 percent of the club if it were to move to Richmond. Dunn made one more attempt to save his team. He made an appeal to the National Commission, the three-man group that ran baseball before there was a single baseball commissioner. Dunn asked the commission to ban the recruiting of International League players by major-league teams, and he even hoped the panel might agree to promote the International League to major-league status. Dunn told the commission:

> I dug deep this season, and I gave Baltimore a team that I
> believe is as strong as a second-division major-league team, if

not stronger. I paid men . . . major-league salaries so that they would be satisfied to play in the International League. To keep them in line, I signed most of them for three years. That makes me personally responsible to them for their salaries for that length of time. I allowed for Federal League sentiment at the beginning of the season, but the novelty has worn off now and Baltimore is still not patronizing the Orioles. Why? Not because the Federals are better, but because the Orioles are in a so-called minor league, and a star player developed there can be taken away by draft and never be seen in Baltimore again. That's what I've been up against. I gave Baltimore a team that won 13 straight games, and on my thirtieth birthday I played to 150 people. And we were in first place, too.

The commission was not moved and declined Dunn's appeals. Dunn then started to look for buyers interested in some of his best players, which was a common way for managers to keep afloat when money was tight. Within a week, Dunn sold his best players to major-league teams like the Yankees and the Reds. Babe Ruth, pitcher Ernie Shore, and catcher Ben Egan were sold to the Boston Red Sox. The Orioles could not recover with their best players being sold to other clubs, and they finished the season badly. The team moved to Richmond but returned to Baltimore in 1916 after the Federal League folded. Dunn once again had a strong team that won seven straight International League championships, and Ruth was on his way to the major leagues.

Ruth
in the Majors

After less than five months in the minor leagues, Babe Ruth was sent to Boston to play for the Red Sox. He was still very childlike and inexperienced in the world, but he was a far cry from the overwhelmed boy he had been when he arrived in Fayetteville for spring training. Ruth was not headed to the Red Sox as a highly anticipated star. He was just another rookie up from the minors, joining a team that already had many star players, and he had a lot to learn. Bill Carrigan, the Red Sox player/manager, years later told *Boston Record* sportswriter Joe Cashman that "Babe was crude in spots. Every so often he served up a fat pitch or a bad pitch when he shouldn't have."

He was not known for his hitting, either. He had come to pitch. In his own words, from his 1928 book, *Babe Ruth's Own Book of Baseball*, he said:

In the Red Sox days, I didn't think much of becoming a slugger. I liked to hit. All fellows do. There isn't a man in baseball who isn't happiest when he's up there at the plate with a stick in his hand. But it was pitching which took my time in Boston. And one of the proudest records I hold to this day is that of having pitched the most consecutive scoreless innings in World Series play.

RUTH ARRIVES IN BOSTON

Ruth got off the train at Boston's Back Bay Station and headed immediately for a nearby diner to have breakfast with his teammates Ernie Shore and Ben Egan. He sat down and began to flirt with his young waitress, Helen Woodford, who was only 16. This is another story that has been debated by some—whether or not the meeting took place on his first day in Boston—but legend has it that it did. What we do know is that Ruth would marry this waitress later that year.

After this chance meeting over breakfast, Ruth, Shore, and Egan headed to Fenway Park, home of the Red Sox since 1912 (the ballpark opened five days after the sinking of the *Titanic*). At the park, the three ballplayers met Carrigan. Carrigan was the Red Sox catcher and had stepped up to be player/manager in the middle of the 1913 season, when the Sox had a dismal record and found themselves in fifth place in the American League. Carrigan was a well-respected and successful manager who impressed Ruth, Shore, and Egan on their first meeting. Throughout his career, Ruth said that Carrigan was the best manager he had ever worked for.

COMPETING FOR A STARTING SPOT

On July 11, 1914, Ruth joined the sixth-place Red Sox. Carrigan had two new pitchers—Ruth and Shore—and wanted to try them out. He gave Ruth the first shot. On his first day in Boston, Ruth played his first major-league game against the Cleveland Indians. He had a notable play in his very first

Babe Ruth and Helen Woodford are shown in their 1914 wedding photo. According to legend, the Babe met Helen on the day he arrived in Boston to join the Red Sox. They were married only three months after they met—he was 19, and she was 16.

inning as pitcher. With a runner on second base, Cleveland's Joe Jackson (known as "Shoeless Joe") came up to bat. Jackson hit a solid single to center field. The runner on second made it to third and briefly rounded the base until deciding to hold there. The center fielder, seeing the runner round third, threw the ball to home plate to prevent the runner from scoring. From the pitcher's mound, Ruth saw that the runner was stopping at third. He promptly caught the ball that had been thrown home—in baseball, this is known as a "cutoff" play—and threw the ball to second, where he could see Jackson was heading. Jackson turned back to first base. When the ball was thrown to first, the runner at third base decided to head home. The first baseman then threw the ball home, and

☆ ☆ ☆ ☆ ☆ ☆

WHAT MAKES FENWAY UNIQUE

Fenway Park was built in 1912 during what is called the "golden age" of baseball parks. Parks built between 1909 and 1915 shared similar characteristics: They were built downtown in a convenient location; seats were arranged to be as close to the field as possible to provide the best views; and these parks had more seating capacity than earlier parks of the day. By today's standards, however, Fenway Park is hardly spacious—it is one of the smallest ballparks in all of Major League Baseball, with a seating capacity of 38,805. Fenway is one of the most recognizable ballparks, and it is the oldest park still used for professional play.

One of the most recognizable features at Fenway, if not in all of sports, is the "Green Monster," the 37-foot-high (11-meter-high) wall in left field. The wall is necessary because of where the park was built, which is right in the middle of the busy Fenway neighborhood of Boston. Because Fenway was built around the runner was tagged out. The play ended with one runner out and the other at first base. In the *Boston Globe* the next day, sportswriter Tim Murane wrote, "The Red Sox pulled off a clever play in the first when Graney lost a fine chance for scoring. Ruth was strong in the play."

Ruth was taken out of the game and replaced by star pitcher Hubert "Dutch" Leonard in the seventh inning. Ruth left the game with the Red Sox winning 3-1, and Leonard retired all the batters he faced in the remaining innings to save the game. Although Ruth had his first major-league victory, he was not as

☆ ☆ ☆ ☆ ☆ ☆

existing streets, there was only room for 315 feet (96 meters) between home plate and the left-field wall—that is about 30 feet (9 meters) less than the minimum distance typically allowed. The wall compensates for the shorter distance, making it hard to knock a ball out of the park.

The Green Monster was erected during a renovation in 1934, when it replaced a 10-foot (3-meter) sloping mound on which the left-field fence stood. The left fielder would have to run up and down this hill during play, and it was called "Duffy's Cliff" after the first left fielder to play in Fenway.

Another rare feature of Fenway Park is its scoreboard, which is still operated by hand. It is one of only two such scoreboards in Major League Baseball today. (The other is at Wrigley Field in Chicago.) Although Fenway is aged and small, Bostonians have fought to keep it open, in a time when many historic parks have been torn down and replaced by larger, more modern stadiums.

strong as Carrigan had hoped. Ruth also had little luck getting a hit that day, striking out and hitting a pop fly in his two at-bats.

Carrigan then gave Shore his shot, and Shore seemed more up to the challenge than Ruth. In his first major-league win, also against the Indians, Shore led the Red Sox to a 2-1 victory, with the Indians getting only two hits off him in the entire game. Ruth had his next chance against the Detroit Tigers, but again he did not impress his new manager, who pulled Ruth from the game and blamed him for the Red Sox's loss. Shore was given another chance to start a game, and again he pitched beautifully. Shore was a right-handed pitcher, which was also good for Carrigan. The team's other right-handed pitchers were erratic, while the two best pitchers were left-handed. Ruth was put on the bench.

SPECULATING WHY RUTH DID NOT PLAY

Fans still wonder if two games were enough for Carrigan to give up on Babe or if there were other reasons. One possible cause, which made the rounds in baseball legend, is that Ruth had a habit of making a gesture with his tongue that indicated when he would throw a curveball. Others blame his behavior. Although he was a professional ballplayer with a reputation for kindness, he was still quite rough around the edges. He was loud and laid-back in a way that annoyed his team-mates—he was a bit of a show-off. These traits would make him popular with the fans, but his Red Sox teammates did not much care for him.

If Ruth felt this cold reception from his team at the time, he forgave it later. Again in his 1928 book about baseball, Ruth recalled his experience with the Red Sox and his teammates, and his manager in particular, as a big break for him and a wonderful learning opportunity:

> Going to the Red Sox was a great break. In those days the Red
> Sox were as much kings of the baseball walk as the Yankees

are today. Then I was on the same club as Bill Carrigan, one of the finest chaps I ever knew, and one of the best coaches of young pitchers there is in the game. With the Red Sox I really began to learn a little baseball. Joe Wood, Dutch Leonard, Ernie Shore, Hugh Bedient, George Foster—what an array it was! And chaps, all of them, who not only knew how to pitch themselves, but fellows who could teach others as well.

Whatever the reason, Ruth sat on the bench throughout a Red Sox road trip to Cleveland, Chicago, St. Louis, and Detroit. Ruth did not pitch a single inning, not even as a relief pitcher for starters who were tiring or having a bad day. Carrigan did not even bring Ruth in to pinch-hit. Almost a month after his second opportunity against the Tigers, Ruth finally pitched in an exhibition game against the minor-league Lawrence, Massachusetts, team, part of the New England League. Ruth won the game 6-4. He won another exhibition game against a New England League team soon after, which at least made him feel hopeful that he was a contributing member of the Red Sox.

PLAYING IN THE MINORS

During the time that Ruth was struggling to find his place, both on the field and off, Joseph Lannin, the owner of the Red Sox, purchased a minor-league team in Providence, Rhode Island. The Providence team had recently lost two of its starting pitchers—one to the major leagues and one to the Federal League. Lannin agreed to send a pitcher down from the Red Sox to pitch for Providence. It was decided that Ruth would be that pitcher.

In those days, a team owner could not move a player from the majors back to the minors without first allowing other major-league teams a shot at acquiring the player. When Garry Herrmann, the owner of the Cincinnati Reds, expressed his interest in bringing Ruth to his team, Lannin fought hard to get around the rule. He did not want to lose Ruth forever; he wanted to help his new venture, the Providence team, and still cash in on his investment—Babe Ruth, for whom he had paid a handsome sum—when Ruth was more ready to play in the majors. Lannin got Ban Johnson, the American League president, to support him in his opposition to the rule. In a letter to Herrmann, Johnson wrote that Lannin had paid a lot for Ruth and had the right to send him to the minors to gather experience. "Under no circumstances will Boston release Pitcher Ruth to a major league club. Mr. Lannin paid an extravagant price for this young man and hopes to develop him. He is unable to give him work at Boston and by sending him to Providence he will have an opportunity to improve the team and possibly make some money." Lannin, too, wrote to Herrmann, focusing on the idea that he wanted to send Ruth to Providence primarily to give him more experience and only secondarily to help his newly acquired team. Herrmann finally gave up on his effort to acquire Ruth.

THE BABE GOES TO PROVIDENCE

Ruth was very displeased with the decision to send him to Providence. It was not entirely as if he were being sent back to the minors: He still earned a major-league salary and still was technically a member of the Boston Red Sox. Nonetheless, the transfer was a blow to the young rookie's ego. On top of that, the move took him away from his girlfriend, Helen, the waitress whom he met on his first day in Boston (as the story goes). Providence was only about 50 miles (80 kilometers) from Boston, and Ruth did find a way to return to see Helen as often as he could.

Ruth's new manager was Wild Bill Donovan. Donovan was excited to have a new left-handed pitcher to serve as a counterpart to Carl Mays, his right-handed pitching ace. Mays had an unusual pitching style, throwing the ball nearly

During his first season with the Red Sox, Babe Ruth was sent down to the minor leagues to play for the Providence Grays. He was not happy with the move, but he was able to pitch more often than he did with the Sox. In six weeks with the Grays, Ruth had a 9–3 record, and he helped lead the team to the pennant.

underarm in such a way that he sometimes scraped his knuckles on the mound when delivering the pitch. Mays and Ruth were alike in that they were both big personalities. They differed in style, however—Ruth was more playful and laid-back while Mays was more aggressive and tough. The two did not get along.

Ruth may have been insulted by the move to Providence, but it seemed to be a great place for him. He got much more playing time than he did with the Red Sox, and he was able to hone his skills and develop more of a crowd-drawing reputation. His team—the Providence Grays, also called the Clamdiggers—were in the pennant race, and Ruth had the opportunity to pitch often. In his six weeks in Providence, he won nine games and lost three and had a .300 batting average. In Toronto, he hit his first home run as a professional ball-player. His team won the pennant, and then Ruth headed back to Boston. The Red Sox were not quite finished with their season, although it was pretty clear they would end up in second place, behind the Philadelphia Athletics. Ruth pitched in two games at the end of the season. He won one and lost one, and so ended his first year in professional baseball. He also proposed to Helen upon his return to Boston. Helen accepted, though they had only known each other three months—during which time Ruth was mostly in Providence. When the season ended, Ruth and Helen returned to Baltimore, where they stayed with Ruth's father.

Ruth was under 21 and therefore had to get his father's permission to marry. Helen, most who were familiar with her believe, must have eloped, as she came from a rather strict Catholic family that would probably not have allowed their teenage daughter, a "good girl" by all accounts, to run away with an unrefined ballplayer to Baltimore.

On October 17, 1914, Babe Ruth and Helen Woodford were married at St. Paul's Catholic Church in Ellicott City, Maryland, a town outside of Baltimore. He was 19, and she was 16. A reception followed in an apartment above the bar that Ruth's father still owned and managed in Baltimore, and it was there that Helen and Babe Ruth spent the first winter of their marriage.

Ruth's Rising Star

Because he thought he was born in 1894, Babe Ruth believed he had turned 21 in February 1915. He was a married man, a professional baseball player, and was now completely independent from his legal guardian at St. Mary's. A month later, he reported for spring training in Hot Springs, Arkansas, and a month after that, Ruth and the rest of the Red Sox traveled to Memphis, Tennessee, to play preseason exhibition games. After those games were over, he and Helen moved to an apartment in Cambridge, Massachusetts, and got ready for the official season to start.

Ruth had proven his talent and worth during his stint in Providence, but he was still not considered the Red Sox's top pitcher. He ranked behind his more experienced and seasoned teammates, Ray Collins, Ernie Shore, Rube Foster, and Dutch

Leonard as well as his fellow rookie and former Providence teammate, Carl Mays. About a month or so into the season, injuries and poor outings seemed to be striking the pitchers that Bill Carrigan, the manager, so heavily counted on. Collins, Shore, and Leonard all pitched badly at the start of the season. Mays's pitching was strong, but a twisted ankle—which he suffered in the second game of the season—knocked him out of play for nearly a month. This proved to be Ruth's big opportunity.

RUTH THE STARTER

Babe Ruth was the starting pitcher in the Red Sox's third game of the 1915 season. He pitched badly and was pulled from the game. With Mays injured and the rest of the staff pitching poorly, however, Carrigan had few options when it came to relief pitchers, and Ruth was given more chances to pitch. Ruth pitched well and was given another chance to start. He won that game, 9-2. The next game he pitched helped to establish Ruth as a major-league pitcher even more so, even though he lost the game. It was against the New York Yankees. Ruth pitched 13 innings in the game, which the Red Sox lost 4-3. His performance impressed Carrigan, and Ruth was finally moved from the bench into the pitching rotation. He could still pitch wildly on some days, though, which made him a bit of a gamble. Before the 1915 season began, sportswriter Paul Shannon of the *Boston Post* wrote, "[Ruth] possesses a wonderful arm and a world of stuff, strength galore, and overwhelming eagerness to be in the game. The Red Sox have a splendid prospect, but one who lacks a knowledge of real 'inside baseball.' Manager Carrigan is confident that he can teach him, and if so he will be a great acquisition to the corps."

Also, Ruth grabbed some attention for hitting his first major-league home run in a game against the Yankees—although he was a few years away from making a name for

Babe Ruth was just one of several stellar pitchers on the Boston Red Sox. Here, some of the members of the pitching staff gathered for a photograph before a game in the 1915 World Series. They were *(from left)* Rube Foster, Carl Mays, Ernie Shore, Ruth, and Dutch Leonard.

himself as a hitter. (Pitchers are not traditionally looked upon for their hitting skills. They also do not play every game, and so do not make it to the plate as often as other players.) A home run in 1915 was not considered a big deal. Historically, this was part of baseball's Dead Ball Era, which is said to have lasted from 1900 until Ruth himself changed the game around 1920. During this period, home runs were not thought to be important. The number of home runs was not listed in the newspapers as part of a player's statistics. A home run was considered, as Robert W. Creamer says in his book, *Babe: The Legend Comes to Life*, "not an occasion for exploding score-boards—or even handshakes." Creamer goes on to liken a home run of 1915 to a "bases-empty triple in the sixth inning of a one-sided game" today.

Home runs were not common then, in part because they were considered a fluke, something that was not done on pur-pose. At the time, baseball was considered more a game of strat-egy—strategy that included stealing bases and hit-and-run plays. Games were far more low-scoring then, and batting averages were lower than today. Another factor of this period was the ball itself, which was not replaced during a game as it is now. After about 100 pitches, the ball would start to unravel, get softer, and be harder to hit with enough power to make it soar like a new ball. Ruth's first home run against the Yankees did make an impression, though, simply because of how far he was able to hit the ball with little perceived effort. Still, in 1915, Ruth's contri-bution to the Red Sox was his pitching, not his hitting.

THE 1915 WORLD SERIES

The 1915 Red Sox were a powerful team. By the end of July, the team was in first place. The Red Sox were great in the field and, mostly, on the mound. Ruth was becoming a first-rate pitcher—he was winning games, though he sometimes tired in the late innings. Ruth, however, was one of six excel-lent pitchers on the team, so he did not stand out as much. He finished the season with a record of 18–8, and he was one of five Red Sox pitchers with 15 wins or more. The team, which had a record of 101–50, made it to the World Series in 1915 and faced the Philadelphia Phillies. Although the Red Sox won the World Series that year, Ruth was not much of a factor. In fact, Ruth's only participation was to pinch-hit

With his 1915 World Series bonus, Babe Ruth bought his father a new bar in Baltimore and worked there during the off-season. Tending bar at Ruth's Café on December 27, 1915, were the Babe *(second from right)* and his father, George Herman Ruth, Sr. *(right)*.

one time in the first game and earn the team its second out of the inning.

When the Series was over, Babe and Helen Ruth—along with the $3,780.25 bonus he received for being part of the World Champion team—returned to Baltimore for the winter. Ruth was known for his generosity as much as his boorishness, and with his windfall, he bought his father a new bar and then worked there until it was time for the 1916 season to begin.

STILL ROUGH AROUND THE EDGES

Ruth's teammates were still struggling to get used to him. Simply put, Ruth was unrefined. He lacked the table manners, etiquette, and hygiene that his teammates expected a grown man to have. He was loud, played jokes that annoyed his teammates, and did not seem to take much seriously. On the road, players did not want to be stuck rooming with Ruth because of his behavior and habits. He was making a lot of money, and he enjoyed spending it. Ruth would drop his suitcase off in his hotel room and immediately go out for the night, spending money on drinking (although he was not yet as heavy a drinker as he would become), gambling, and looking for women. It got so that Carrigan would arrange to have the hotel room next to Ruth's when the team was on the road. Ruth's behavior off the field got increasingly worse. He drank more and fought often with his manager about the curfew imposed on the players while the team was on the road. Eventually, Ruth had to write notes to his manager telling him what time he got in the night before.

Helen, Ruth's wife, was not any less of an outsider. She was shy and awkward and had difficulty relating to the other players' wives. She also seemed not to understand the full scope of her husband's fame, reacting with surprise when strangers recognized him on the street. The low opinion that the other wives had of Ruth did not help Helen get along any better with them. Ken Sobol, author of *Babe Ruth and the American Dream*, spoke many years later with wives of Ruth's teammates and other athletes about what they remembered of the man. What they said was not flattering. "He was a mess. He was foulmouthed, a show-off, very distasteful to have around," recalled Margaret Gardner, wife of Red Sox player Larry Gardner. "The kind of person you would never dream of having over to dinner. I suppose he was likable enough in his own way, but you couldn't prove it by me."

Grace Monroe, who was married to a famous Boston boxer and had encountered Ruth, said of him:

> I doubt that he appealed to many women. He certainly didn't appeal to me. He was so blustery and loud. And he used so many swear words it embarrassed you. And believe me, I don't embarrass easy. He didn't ever seem to want to be with women anyway. He'd always rather be with the men, talking about fighting or something like that. Somebody I knew who knew him real well used to say he was a "man's man." Well, he certainly wasn't a woman's man—I don't care how many women he slept with.

For his part, Ruth had this to say of people's impressions of ballplayers—and perhaps a little in defense of himself—in *Babe Ruth's Own Book of Baseball*:

> A lot of people still cling to the idea that professional base-ball players are roughnecks, hardly fit to associate with real folks. And of course there are good fellows and bad, among the players. But then the same thing might be said of lawyers or doctors or businessmen. Believe me, playing side by side with a man through season after season, living with him in hotels, traveling with him on the road, eating and sleeping with him month after month, gives a fellow a pretty good line on just what sort of fellow he is.
>
> And I say to you that in my experience I've found ball-players to be just as much gentlemen as any class of men I ever knew. Nine times out of ten they're a lot better than the people who criticize them.

THE 1916 RED SOX

Ruth reported to spring training, his frame now supporting all 212 pounds (96 kilograms) of him. His pitching had become more consistent than it was his rookie year. Mays, his fellow rookie from the 1915 season, was also in great form, and Shore, Foster, and Leonard continued to be among the best pitchers in the league. The team lost its best hitter to another team because of a salary dispute, however, and the Red Sox were fairly weak at the plate.

This was the year that Babe Ruth began to stand out, as a pitcher and a personality, but also as a hitter. With their best hitter gone, the Red Sox badly needed someone who could be sure to knock in runs. Ruth had hit home runs, which went largely uncelebrated, and had a fine batting average, but because he was a pitcher, he had fewer opportunities at bat than other players. At the start of the 1916 season, Carrigan began to wonder what would happen if he put Babe Ruth in the outfield and let him play more games, giving him more chances to hit. It was just a thought at this stage, though, and Ruth continued to pitch. And pitch he did. Ruth finished the season with a record of 23–12, and he had a league-leading earned-run average of 1.75. "No pitcher in baseball, certainly no left-handed pitcher, was better," Leigh Montville wrote of Ruth's season. "He could throw a fastball past anyone, including the feared Ty Cobb."

The Red Sox had a great season, too, and once more made it to the World Series, this time against the Brooklyn Robins (later the Dodgers). In this Series, Ruth got to play. Carrigan put him in to pitch in the second game. It was the only game in which Ruth played, but he gave a tremendous performance, defeating the Robins 2-1 in an exciting 14-inning game. Ruth pitched the entire game. The Sox went on to win the World Series for the second year in a row.

BASEBALL IN THE SHADOW OF WORLD WAR I

As the 1916 season came to a close, team owners across baseball were continuing to be economical, starting players at lower salaries, limiting raises, and in many cases, cutting salaries. (The demise of the Federal League the year before

Babe Ruth had a breakout year in 1916, finishing the season with an ERA of 1.75—best in the American League. His hitting also began to attract some notice. The Red Sox again won the World Series, with Ruth pitching them to a win in a 14-inning game.

had created a surplus of major-league-caliber players, giving the owners more leverage in contract negotiations.) One of the very few raises that Harry Frazee, the new owner of the Red Sox, permitted was a relatively low raise of $1,500 for Babe Ruth, bringing his salary to $5,000 per year. Ruth appreciated the circumstances and took this raise without argument. Ruth arrived at spring training in 1917, and the team was generally upbeat. It was becoming more and more likely, however, that the United States would enter World War I, and on April 6, 1917, by a vote of 82 to 6 in the Senate and 373 to 50 in the House of Representatives, the United States of America declared war on Germany.

Officials in Major League Baseball in general worried about the status of its players now that the country was at war. Would star players be drafted into military service, and if so, what would this do to baseball? Team owners and managers instituted military drills during practices and before games. At the first game of the 1917 season, the Red Sox marched before play started. The drills were implemented, one baseball official said at the time, because "it has been indicated that it will be the policy of the War Department to leave undisturbed in their occupations all men who may be subject to service if they are receiving military instruction."

In May, however, the Selective Service Act of 1917 was passed. The act obligated all men ages 21 to 30 to sign up for the draft. Most baseball players who did sign up, however, were not sent overseas. Many stayed in the United States doing jobs that were intended to keep up morale, such as coaching and training teams. Ruth had registered for the draft, but he would be exempt from service because of his marital status.

RUTH BECOMES A CELEBRITY

Ruth began the 1917 season aware of his star status with the Boston Red Sox, which fed his ego and led to some behavior problems on the field. Ruth began to argue more and more with the umpires when he disagreed with a call. During a home game at Fenway Park against Washington on June 23, Ruth lashed out at an umpire after the umpire called four balls and walked a batter. In Ruth's own words: "I just went crazy. I rushed up to the plate and I said, 'If you'd go to bed at night, you so-and-so, you could keep your eyes open long enough in the daytime to see when a ball goes over the plate.'" The argument went on a little longer and then, as Ruth told it, "I hauled off and hit him—right on the jaw. Chet Thomas, our catcher, [Jack] Barry [the new team manager], and other players tore us apart and hustled me to the clubhouse." Ruth was tossed from the game and banned from play for 10 days, fined a very lenient $100 by league president Ban Johnson, and made to apologize in the papers for his actions.

This behavior earned him criticism from some sports columnists, but mostly it enhanced his celebrity. Ruth appeared more and more in the sports pages, and his personal life—such as his decision to buy a country home—was covered in detail in other sections of the papers as well.

The 1917 season ended with the Red Sox in second place behind the Chicago White Sox. The Red Sox had won 90 games and lost 62. Ruth himself had won 24 and lost 13. He also batted .325—not bad for a pitcher with limited at-bats—and it was at the end of the season that some of his teammates started to say that perhaps Ruth would be more valuable as an everyday player, when he would have more opportunities to hit, than as a left-handed pitcher.

A SEASON CLOUDED BY WAR AND FLU

The Red Sox had lost some players to the draft—13 in all—including Jack Barry, their player/manager who had replaced Carrigan in 1917. Harry Frazee hired Ed Barrow to manage the Red Sox. From the start of the 1918 season, Ruth was a problem for the new manager, disobeying orders and once threatening to punch him in the nose. Ruth also saw himself as more valuable as an everyday player rather than a pitcher, claiming he could "win more games playing every day in the outfield than I will pitching every fourth day." Barrow felt strongly that Ruth should continue as a pitcher, but because of a string of poor performances by the Red Sox first basemen, Ruth was given his first shot at playing first base in a major-league game on May 6. He played beautifully, performing well on the field and hitting a home run. Ruth played first base for another couple of games and continued to please the crowd with his hitting. Still, Barrow considered him a pitcher first.

Then on May 23, baseball received another blow when a new ruling of "work or fight" was announced by Secretary of War Newton Baker. This declared that all men ages 21 to 30 must either be drafted or working in some capacity in a war-related enterprise. It was clear this time that baseball players were not exempt, although some performers—actors, singers—were. To quote the "work or fight" ruling, it applied to "persons, including ushers and other attendants, engaged in and occupied in and in connection with, games, sports, and amusements, excepting actual performers in legitimate concerts, operas or theatrical performances."

When this new policy was announced, Ruth was not in the Red Sox lineup. He was suffering from the flu. A new threat would hit the country in a few months: It was called Spanish influenza, a sickness that traveled from the war trenches back to the United States with returning soldiers, and which quickly became an epidemic. (It is unknown if Ruth had the same strain of flu as the Spanish influenza.)

RUTH EMERGES AS A HITTER

Ruth went to Fenway Park on his day to pitch, but he was clearly too sick to play when he arrived. He was hurried to the hospital, where he stayed for a week. Following his release from the hospital, Ruth pitched and lost a game, but hit a home run. In the next game, he played center field and hit another home run. He hit four home runs in four straight games after nearly dying from the flu. Ruth continued to push to be made a full-time player rather than a pitcher. His illness actually helped Ruth's cause in this respect: While he was out, Barrow had to find a replacement for him, and he chose pitcher Sam Jones, who did rather well. Ruth and Barrow came to an agreement that Ruth would play center field in some games and pitch in others, and for playing two positions, Ruth got a

★ ★ ★ ★ ★ ☆
THE 1918 INFLUENZA EPIDEMIC

The influenza epidemic (which was called the Spanish influenza epidemic, although it did not originate in Spain) affected more than half the world's population, according to author G. Beatty Marks. Worldwide, it reportedly killed 20 million to 40 million people, and possibly as many as 50 million people, making it the worst pandemic in history. In the United States, an estimated 500,000 to 675,000 people died from the disease in just about a year before it disappeared. The disease was extremely contagious and deadly, affecting mostly young adults.

The epidemic was not received with as much alarm and media coverage as you might expect. According to the November 5, 1918, issue of the *New York Times*, this reaction was in part because "war had taught the people to think in terms other than the individual interest and safety, and death itself had become so familiar as to lose its grimness." The flu and the war became almost one and the same with the American people at the time, blurring together the list of war victims and those who died from influenza.

$1,000 bonus. The Red Sox, against odds presented by the draft and the flu, won the pennant in 1918, and went on to play in the World Series, beating the Chicago Cubs. Because of the "work or fight" ruling, the shortened 1918 season ended on Labor Day. Players, managers, and owners alike, though, were just happy to have been able to finish the season at all.

Amid threats of the 1919 season being canceled, players were concerned for their future. Attendance was down at the World Series. Ticket prices had been cut, which also lowered the gate receipts. The players on both teams actually threatened a strike in the middle of the World Series over the amount of money they would receive. Still, the series went on, and the Red Sox took it four games to two. It was the fourth World Series win for the Red Sox, more than any other team at the time, but it would be their last for 86 years. Then, two months after the World Series, World War I was over.

Ruth the Controversial Celebrity

With World War I over and a new season about to begin, Babe Ruth, aware of his rising celebrity status and living more and more extravagantly, was poised to press for more money. He was the star player of the star team, a team that had won a remarkable three World Series in the previous four years, and he was ready to push for what he felt he was worth: $15,000 per year, which was a grand leap from his 1918 salary of $7,000. Red Sox owner Harry Frazee quickly said no way.

The Red Sox owner was in a tough spot economically. The more he paid his players, the more he had to count on money from ticket sales to keep the Red Sox a profitable organization. Frazee had even more financial problems because of investments he had made in the theater—theater was his true passion, and he owned theaters and produced plays, all of which were losing money. At the start of the 1919 season, Frazee was more interested in selling players to make money than he was on buying players or giving substantial raises to current players.

Frazee stood his ground. He met with Babe Ruth in person only once to discuss Ruth's salary, and after that the two men communicated only through the press. Ruth threatened to quit baseball over the dispute. Frazee laughed off the claim, sure that the Babe could not live without playing baseball. Ruth demanded a salary of $15,000 a year or a three-year contract at $10,000 a year. Frazee countered with an offer of $8,500 per year. Ruth raised his demands to include how he would be used on the team, saying that he did not want to both pitch and play the outfield, but only to play the outfield full time. In the end, Ruth got a three-year contract for $10,000 a year, and the battle was over.

Ruth never made any apologies in asking for raises. He said:

> It isn't right to call me or any ballplayer an ingrate because we ask for more money. Sure I want more, all I'm entitled to. The time of the ballplayer is short. He must get his money in a few years or lose out. Listen, a man who works for another is not going to get any more than he's worth. You can bet on that. A man ought to get all he can earn. A man who knows he's making the money for other people ought to get some of the profit he brings in. Don't make any difference if it's baseball or a bank or a vaudeville show. It's business, I tell you. There ain't no sentiment to it. Forget that stuff.

Ruth was more or less a full-time outfielder throughout the 1919 season. Of the 130 games in which Ruth played, he only pitched in 17. He hit 29 home runs—which was then the major-league record for a single season. He hit a home run in

Babe Ruth was used more and more as an everyday player during the 1919 season, his last one with the Red Sox. Of the 130 games he played that year, he pitched in only 17 of them. In 1919, Ruth set a new season record for home runs with 29. He would break his own record in each of the next two seasons.

every ballpark in the American League. It was not a good year, though, for the Sox: The team finished in sixth place with 66 wins and 71 losses. Boston's run as World Series champions was over. Ruth's fame grew throughout the season, however, and his off-field behavior worsened. His wife, Helen, spent more and more time alone on a farm the couple had purchased outside of Boston, and Ruth spent more and more time drinking and gambling. His fame had also made him very popular with the many women he would encounter, at home and on the road. He became fatter, more irresponsible, and cockier, being more and more sure of himself as the star of the Red Sox than ever before.

SOLD TO NEW YORK

After the season, Ruth's personal manager, Johnny Igoe, arranged for the celebrity player to visit Los Angeles, where he was to appear in an exhibition golf tournament as well as a string of small films (the films fell through). Before heading to California, Ruth contacted Frazee and threatened to sit out the 1920 season if his contract from 1919—three years for $10,000 a year—was not doubled. "I will not play with the Red Sox until I get $20,000," Ruth said. "I made a bad move last year when I signed a three-year contract to play for $30,000. The Boston club realized much on my value, and I think I am entitled to twice as much as my contract calls for." From California, Ruth claimed to be considering staying out West for good, stating that he had opportunities there that would earn him a great deal more money than he could make in baseball at his current salary.

Meanwhile, Frazee's own financial problems were only getting worse, and he was in no position to meet such a demand. To keep afloat financially, Frazee had begun to sell players to the New York Yankees' owner, Jacob Ruppert. On December 26, 1919, Frazee did what he felt he had to do: He sold Babe Ruth to the Yankees for the unprecedented sum of $125,000. Frazee announced his decision to the press on January 5, indicating that the decision was not just about money but also about Ruth's behavior in general:

> It would be impossible to start the next season with Ruth and have a smooth-working machine. Ruth had become simply impossible, and the Boston club could no longer put up with his eccentricities. I think the Yankees are taking a

gamble. While Ruth is undoubtedly the greatest hitter the game has ever seen, he is likewise one of the most selfish and inconsiderate men ever to put on a baseball uniform. Had he possessed the right disposition, had he been willing to take orders and work for the good of the club like the other men on the team, I never would have dared let him go.

Babe Ruth, meanwhile, was still out West with his wife, basking in the Los Angeles sun. He had no idea that he had just been sold to the New York club. The Yankees' owner did not want the announcement made until he was sure how Ruth would react. Miller Huggins, the Yankees' manager, was sent to California to break the news. Ruth began to make salary demands, and eventually a contract was settled: Ruth got the $20,000 a year for two years that he had been demanding.

☆ ☆ ☆ ☆ ☆ ☆

THE CURSE OF THE BAMBINO

The myth of the "Curse of the Bambino" is that the Red Sox, after selling Babe Ruth to the Yankees, were doomed to never again win a World Series championship—cosmic payback for the sale. Before the sale of Ruth, the Red Sox had won four of the first 15 World Series. After the sale, the Yankees went on to win the Series 26 times by 2006. The phrase first gained widespread use when sportswriter Dan Shaughnessy published a book with that as its title in 1990. Eighty-six years after their 1918 Series victory, the "curse" was finally reversed in 2004, when the Boston Red Sox defeated the St. Louis Cardinals, sweeping them in four games to become World Series champions. Before that victory, the Red Sox had appeared in only four World Series in those 86 years, losing each of them in seven games.

This salary was by far the highest a baseball player had ever received.

New Yorkers, however, generally felt that Ruth would be worth it. Bostonians, meanwhile, were somewhat divided by the decision. Many fans felt that Ruth really had been the strength of the ball club and would leave a gap that the owners could not possibly fill. The *Boston Herald* took a less grim approach: "Stars generally are temperamental," the paper printed. "This goes for baseball and the stage. They often have to be handled with kid gloves. Frazee has carefully considered the Ruth angle and believes he has done the proper thing. Boston fans undoubtedly will be up in arms, but they should reserve judgment until they see how it works out."

RUTH'S START AS A YANKEE

New York City was the place to be in 1920. The city was hopping. Although the recent Eighteenth Amendment had instituted Prohibition, making alcohol illegal in the United States, all over New York City were secret bars, called speakeasies, where the liquor flowed and Ruth made himself at home. In New York City, a famed player like Ruth would find himself more celebrated than he could ever have been in Boston. Still, Ruth had to prove himself worthy of the great investment the Yankees had just made in him, and he showed up for spring training in great physical condition. As soon as evening came, though, Ruth was in a cab and off for a night on the town.

Ruth began his first season as a Yankee as a center fielder. He did not get off to a fantastic start, either in the field or at the plate. As the year went on, Ruth's performance improved, and by the end of the 1920 season, Ruth had a landmark batting record: 54 home runs, 9 triples, 36 doubles, 158 runs scored, 137 runs batted in, 14 stolen bases, and an overall batting average of .376. He led the league in home runs, RBIs, and runs scored. In fact, his home-run total of 54 beat out 14 of the other 15 major-league teams. The presence of the Babe

In a game during his first year with the New York Yankees, Babe Ruth gets a hit against his old team, the Red Sox. In 1920 and 1921, his first two years as a Yankee, Ruth had phenomenal seasons at the plate—shattering his old home-run record and changing the way the game was played.

had also caused an increase in attendance at Yankee games. Attendance at home games had more than doubled—from 619,164 in 1919 to 1,289,422 in 1920. The season did not end in a championship—the Yankees came in third in the American League—but Ruth's debut as a Yankee had been a great success.

If the 1920 season had been a good one for Ruth, the 1921 season was certainly his best ever. His batting record surpassed that of the previous year, with 59 home runs, 16 triples, 44 doubles, 204 hits, and an overall batting average of .378. The 1921 Yankees were a strong team in general and finished the season with a record of 98 wins and 55 losses, good enough to win the American League title. In the World Series, the Yankees faced another New York ball club, the New York Giants. Ruth had a strong Series but was taken out of play for two games because of injuries. The Yankees lost the World Series in the end, but Ruth and his team had made a strong showing, and the season and Series were both celebrated. The year was special in other ways as well, as the Ruths adopted a baby girl, Dorothy.

THE LIVE BALL ERA

This period was a time of change for baseball as whole—it marked the end of the Dead Ball Era. Something that we perhaps take for granted about modern-day baseball is that it is a game fueled by powerful hitters who are often the most popular and best-paid players. This view of baseball can be directly attributed to Ruth. Before Ruth's time, baseball was far more a game of defensive strategy, with teams focusing and relying on savvy pitching and solid fielding to prevent the other team from scoring rather than approaching the game more offensively by relying on strong batters to score runs.

In the early 1900s leading up to Ruth's first major-league home run in 1915, baseball games had far lower scores on average and batting averages were notably different, averaging around .250 for major-league players. That average increased to .285 in 1921.

After World War I, baseball entered what is called the "lively ball" period, or Live Ball Era, which takes its name from the mistaken idea that batting averages increased because a new type of ball had been developed—the lively ball. In fact, baseballs were being manufactured the same way they had always been. Instead of one ball being used for most of game, however,

Before a game in 1922 at Fenway Park, Babe Ruth frolicked with his daughter, Dorothy, on the field. His wife had brought their daughter to Boston to spend a few days with Ruth. Increasingly, their marriage was a tense one, and Helen Ruth withdrew more and more to the family's farm in Massachusetts.

balls were now being replaced. This helped power hitters, as did a ban on tricky pitches, like the spitball.

Attendance at baseball games rose steadily after the war, and Ruth was one of the main draws. People began to focus on the excitement of high-scoring games. People wanted to see the Babe hit home runs. Coaches were happy to oblige. With fans wanting to see big hits and big innings, the very strategy of the game changed as a result of Ruth's power at bat.

1922: A TURN FOR THE WORSE

Babe Ruth had completed two very successful seasons with the New York Yankees, but after the 1921 World Series, Ruth's own stubbornness and arrogance again tripped him up, and his good fortune took a turn. This slide was a result of a rule that prohibited players who had been in the World Series from participating in any off-season exhibition games. Ruth had always enjoyed these barnstorming games—in large part because he made so much money playing in them. Ruth ignored the rule, despite warnings from the baseball commissioner, and left on an exhibition tour almost immediately after the 1921 Series. For this, Ruth was suspended from play for the first six weeks of the 1922 season. Ruth was suspended again three more times during the season for arguing with umpires.

His personal life was not faring any better. Helen, long out of place in the celebrity lifestyle in which Ruth so thrived, retreated more and more from the spotlight and from Ruth. Helen and daughter Dorothy were living on their farm in Massachusetts while Ruth, alone in New York City, continued to indulge in food and alcohol and affairs with many women.

The 1922 season once again ended with the Yankees facing the Giants—and losing—in the World Series. Ruth knew he would have to prove his worth in the coming year, and he spent the winter getting into shape for the 1923 season.

ENDEARING TO HIS FANS

For all the trouble Ruth had with his managers, colleagues, wives of other players, and so on, he was adored by the public. Ruth had a close connection to his fans, always responding to their letters—even while hospitalized—and taking time to sign autographs and shake hands. He was even willing to humor the oddball request, such as the one from a fan who asked Ruth, in a letter, for a lock of his hair. Ruth agreed to this request, if only because of its unusual nature. The letter

Babe Ruth offered up a few tips to some of his young fans in 1924 in New York. Ruth may have had problems with his teammates or managers, but the fans adored him.

Ruth wrote to this fan, which is on display at the Babe Ruth Museum in his hometown of Baltimore, said:

> Dear Mathew,
>
>   In all my years in baseball, I have received many requests for autographs, bats, balls, and equipment, but you are the first person to ask me for some of my hair. Therefore I feel I am obliged to comply with such a request at least once. You will find enclosed an envelope containing some of my hair. I don't know what you're going to do with it, but I hope you enjoy it. Good luck with your collection.
>   Sincerely,
>   Babe Ruth

Ruth had a special connection in particular with the kids who looked up to him, although these stories do often get exaggerated to mythic proportions. In 1926, he was asked to visit the bedside of a young boy named Johnny Sylvester, who was very sick with some terrible disease. As legend has it, Ruth visited the boy and promised to hit a home run for him in his next game (the Yankees were playing in the 1926 World Series). Ruth hit three home runs, and the boy got better. In Robert W. Creamer's biography of Babe Ruth, he tells the real story: Johnny Sylvester had actually fallen from a horse and had no disease. To cheer the boy up, a friend of the family brought him some baseballs autographed by the Yankees and the Cardinals just before that year's World Series along with a promise from Ruth that he would hit a home run for him. Ruth did visit Johnny Sylvester, but after the Series, in which he had hit four home runs. A year later, when the boy's uncle thanked Ruth for his visit, Ruth said no problem, then turned to a sportswriter he had been sitting with and asked who Johnny Sylvester was.

6

The House
That Ruth Built

After a disappointing 1922 season for the Yankees and an equally bad year for Babe Ruth on a personal level, the 1923 season offered an opportunity for a fresh start. At a charity dinner in Manhattan shortly after the 1922 World Series, Ruth announced that he would reform himself over the winter:

> I know as well as anybody else just what mistakes I made last season. There's no use in me trying to get away from them. But let me tell you something. I want the New York sportswriters and fans to know that I've had my last drink until next October. I mean it. Tomorrow I am going to my farm. I'm going to work my head off—and maybe part of my stomach.

Ruth emphasized his commitment. "I'm serious about this. I'm going to work hard. And then you just watch me break that home-run record next year." His proclamation was met with great applause. Although Ruth probably did not quit drinking, he obviously worked hard over the winter months and arrived at spring training in 1923 in better shape than his team had seen him in some time. Still a big man—6-foot-2 (188 centimeters) and weighing about 215 pounds (97.5 kilograms)—Ruth started out strong in the first game of the season, with a game-winning home run, and he continued to play well throughout the year.

YANKEE STADIUM

The other fresh start for the Yankees in the 1923 season was the opening of Yankee Stadium. From 1913 until April 1923, the Yankees had to borrow time on the New York Giants' home field, the Polo Grounds. In 1920, after the Yankees outdrew the Giants in attendance, the Giants asked the Yankees to find a new home. The land on which Yankee Stadium was built—10 acres in the Bronx—was purchased by the Yankees in 1921 for $675,000. Yankee Stadium was built in an irregular shape, like a horseshoe, and its shape made the right-field fence shorter than that of center or left field. The shorter right-field fence gave left-handed batters an advantage, because it was easier to hit a home run to right field than anywhere else. Because of their star left-handed batter, right field in the Yankees' new home was called "Ruthsville." Over the years, the park has been renovated, and this problem has largely been corrected.

Yankee Stadium cost $2.5 million to build—a staggering amount at the time, but the results were considered well worth it. It was the first ballpark ever to have triple decks. Although there was some talk of calling it "Ruth Field," the name Yankee Stadium was chosen—the first ballpark ever to be called a

Babe Ruth posed with Yankee batboy Ray Kelly on April 18, 1923—the day of the first game ever played at Yankee Stadium. Ruth hit a home run on that day to guide the Yankees to a 4-1 win over the Red Sox. Yankee Stadium is often called "The House That Ruth Built."

stadium. It was commonly nicknamed "The House That Ruth Built," however, in recognition of Babe Ruth being the major draw for the Yankees at the time the stadium was built.

More than 62,000 fans showed up on Opening Day on April 18, 1923, to watch the Yankees play the Boston Red Sox. The *Baseball Almanac* quotes Ruth as saying before that first game, "I'd give a year of my life if I can hit a home run in the first game in this new park." Sure enough, Ruth hit a three-run homer, and the Yankees won 4-1.

BABE BACK ON TOP

The 1923 season was a great success for Babe Ruth. He achieved the highest batting average of his career—.393—good enough for second in the league behind Harry Heilmann of Detroit, who hit .403. Ruth hit more home runs than anyone else in the major leagues (only 41, which was not Ruth's best, but was still *the* best of the season). Even an accusation in the middle of the season that Ruth was using an illegal bat did not distract from his powerful record at the plate.

Ruth had also changed his behavior considerably since the 1922 season, missing far fewer games (only two, compared with 40 the previous year). The Yankees were strong as a team, too, and easily won the pennant, heading into their third World Series against the Giants. After being injured in the first Series against the Giants and playing poorly in the second, Ruth took

☆ ☆ ☆ ☆ ☆

BANNING THE BETSY BINGLE

In the middle of the 1923 season during a bit of a slump, Babe Ruth was persuaded to try a new bat, nicknamed "the Betsy Bingle." His batting immediately improved, as he got 27 hits in his next 65 at-bats. Regular bats were built from one piece of wood. A batter would hit the ball best if he hit it with the strongest grain of the wood. This new bat was built from four pieces of wood glued together, which made the bat strong all around. The glue was what made the bat illegal, according to the league. Glue increased the velocity of the ball off the bat. Allowing for glue might have opened the door for other materials to be used on bats to improve performance—a practice that is still illegal. In the end, Ruth went back to his old bat and his success at the plate was as strong as ever.

this third face-off as a chance to shine. Ruth played better than anyone in the 1923 Series, hitting .368 with three home runs. The Yankees won, four games to two. It was the first of many World Series wins for the New York Yankees.

The Yankees and Babe Ruth went into and finished the 1924 season strong, although they did not win the pennant that year. The Yankees finished the season with 89 wins and 63 losses, coming in second behind the Washington Senators. Ruth hit .378 to win the only batting title of his career. He also hit 46 home runs, to lead the league again.

BABE'S BELLYACHE

When the 1924 season was over, Ruth set off on an exhibition tour—no longer an illegal practice for professional players—while his wife, Helen, stayed home on their farm outside of Boston. When the tour was over, Ruth joined Helen, but he did not stay very long. The marriage was failing. Helen was suspicious of her husband's activities while he was away from her, which was often. In fact, by this time, he had met and fallen in love with another woman, Claire Hodgson. Still, the couple would not divorce, because they were both Catholic.

Spring training in 1925 brought Ruth a string of problems. To start, he was 20 pounds (9 kilograms) overweight, which affected his play and led to speculation that he was old and fat and his best days were over. His wife and child had joined him for spring training in St. Petersburg, Florida, which took away the freedom he enjoyed when he traveled alone. He broke his finger and had to sit out five games. Then, while on a preseason exhibition tour with the Yankees, Ruth became sicker than he had ever been, suffering stomach cramps and fever. Ruth collapsed in a train station in Asheville, North Carolina, and was rushed back to New York.

News of his collapse spread quickly, and there was plenty of speculation about what had caused Ruth's condition. Some said it was because he was terribly overweight. Others thought

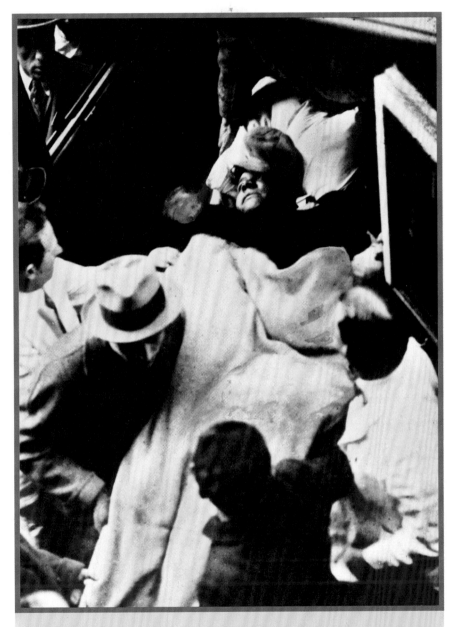

Suffering abdominal pain, Babe Ruth was loaded into an ambulance near Penn Station in New York City in April 1925. He had collapsed in a North Carolina train station and was rushed back to New York. Ruth's mysterious illness came to be known as "the bellyache heard around the world."

he might have contracted a sexually transmitted disease. Others blamed it on drink. The common thread, of course, was that Babe Ruth's lifestyle was to blame. Ruth checked into a hospital for six weeks, where he was allowed few visitors and supervised workouts. The real cause of Ruth's illness, which was called "the bellyache heard around the world," is not known.

The year did not get any better once the official season started. The Yankees finished with 69 wins and 85 losses, second-to-last in the American League. Ruth batted .290, his first season below .300 since he was a pitcher. It was also in 1925 that Babe and Helen Ruth separated.

A COMEBACK AND A RECORD

After a disastrous 1925 season, the Yankees and the Babe came back strong in 1926. Ruth made his intentions for the new year public by printing his resolutions in the *New York Graphic*. They were:

1. To beat his world's record of 59 home runs made in 1921.
2. To observe strictly the training rules laid down by the Yankees.
3. To hold his temper.
4. To be obedient.
5. To be thrifty—no more extravagance.
6. To take part in every one of the 154 games on the schedule.
7. To watch his diet carefully.
8. To conserve his health.
9. To do his share in bringing another pennant to New York.

The team did win the pennant in 1926 but lost to the Cardinals in the World Series. Still, the team and the Babe had managed to overcome what looked like the end of their glory the year before. Ruth did not beat his record, but he again led the league in home runs, with 47. Ruth's closest rival had a mere 19 homers.

And the next year was even better. Many baseball historians say that the 1927 Yankees were the best team of all time. Batting third and fourth in the lineup were Babe Ruth and Lou Gehrig. By June, the papers began to notice that Ruth was on pace to break his 1921 home-run record of 59—that he might hit 60 homers that season. On top of that, he had competition in this quest, from Gehrig. At the end of June, both men were tied with 24 home runs. For the next couple of months, the two sluggers were never more than two home runs apart. The battle continued into early September—Ruth and Gehrig were tied with 44 home runs apiece. Then Ruth went on a tear. With a final three-game series against the Washington Senators left in the season, Ruth only needed three home runs to reach 60. He got two, including a grand slam, in the first game and hit his sixtieth home run in the eighth inning of the second game. Ruth had hit 17 home runs in September, a record for any month. Gehrig had trailed off in September and finished with 47 home runs.

The Yankees ended the season with 110 wins and only 44 losses. The World Series was almost anti-climactic after Ruth's spectacular season, as the Yankees swept the Pittsburgh Pirates in four games.

For all the claims that Babe Ruth was unmanageable, he certainly expressed a lot of respect for his manager, Miller Huggins. As with Brother Matthias, Ruth did listen to men he respected. In his book, *Babe Ruth's Own Book of Baseball*, Ruth recalls that Huggins used Ruth's skills at bat to discourage the Pirates psychologically while the Pirates watched the Yankees practice the day before the World Series began. Huggins told Ruth to step up to the plate and told the pitcher,

Babe Ruth watched the flight of the ball after he struck his record-setting sixtieth home run of the 1927 season on September 30 against the Washington Senators. The 1927 Yankees, who went on to sweep the Pittsburgh Pirates in the World Series, are considered one of the best teams in baseball history.

"When you go in there, lay that ball right down the middle. Don't put anything on it. Let's show those fellows some real hitting!" In Ruth's own words:

Then I came up. Bob [Shawkey] laid them right down the middle, with just enough speed to make them perfect. The first ball I hit right over the roof of the right-field grandstand. I put another one into the lower tier. Then I got a hold of one and laid it in the center-field bleachers.

I was about to quit, but Huggins walked over past me.

"Hit a couple more, Babe," he whispered. "We've got them talking to themselves."

The Pirates were flabbergasted. A friend of mine—one of the newspaper men who was in the stands—heard them talking.

The upshot was that the Pirates left the park that afternoon half-licked before the Series ever opened. They came out to see if we could hit as hard as everybody claimed, and smart little Hug spiked them in the first ten minutes.

The streak continued into 1928, when the Yankees again won the World Series, this time against the St. Louis Cardinals. Twice now in the 1920s, the Yankees had won the American League pennant three times in a row, and they had just won their second straight World Series. The Yankees were the star team in baseball, and Ruth was the star of the Yankees. He was given his own train car in which to travel while his teammates slept on bunks in shared cabins. In the luxury of his own car, wearing his satin smoking jacket and slippers, Babe Ruth relaxed and played his ukulele. In his years as a professional ballplayer, Ruth had evolved from a starry-eyed boy who had never left Baltimore to one of the most traveled players in baseball.

TRAGEDY AND A NEW BEGINNING

By the end of the Yankees' second World Series victory, Ruth was once again drinking heavily, eating gluttonously, and spending money on extravagant amusements, such as a hairless dog from Mexico. As difficult as his behavior could be for his teammates and Helen, from whom he was separated but who undoubtedly still heard rumors of her husband's exploits, the public generally loved him. He was often described as larger than life, energetic, generous with time and money, jolly. Everything he did was over the top. He acted on his impulses, as a child might, without considering consequences.

In January 1929, Helen Ruth was killed in a fire at her home in Massachusetts. Ruth attended the funeral, as did a number of his Yankee teammates. Although Ruth cried when he heard the news and showed sentiment at the funeral, Helen's death did make a new phase of his life possible: Three months later, Babe Ruth married Claire Hodgson. As for the Yankees, they would not win the pennant in 1929, 1930, or 1931.

The Beginning of the End

Following the death of Helen Ruth and Babe Ruth's marriage to Claire Hodgson, Babe Ruth told reporters, "We're not going on a honeymoon. We're going to work and win another pennant." Although the Yankees did not win the pennant in 1929 or for the next two years, Ruth continued to play well, leading or tying for the most home runs in the league every season. The Yankees may have disappointed, but Ruth's home life was on an upswing. Ruth adopted Claire's daughter, Julia, and Claire adopted Ruth's daughter, Dorothy. Claire managed Ruth's financing, distributing money to him and controlling his spending, as well as curbing his eating and drinking.

In 1929, the year they were married, Ruth was in the third year of an impressive $70,000-a-year contract. Although the Yankees were in a slump, Ruth was still in top form. When

In Surrogate's Court in New York City in October 1930, Babe Ruth signed papers to adopt Julia, the daughter of his new wife, Claire. Claire Ruth also adopted Babe Ruth's daughter, Dorothy. With Ruth were *(from left)* Claire Hodgson Ruth, Dorothy Ruth, and Julia Ruth.

it came time to renegotiate his contract for the 1930 season, Ruth pressed for a raise, despite the team's losses and the Great Depression. When he arrived at spring training, he demanded a $100,000 salary, which was rejected outright. Instead, he was offered a $5,000 raise, which Ruth rejected. After much back and forth—during which Ruth threatened to turn in his uniform and quit baseball—Ruth was offered $80,000 a year for two years, and he accepted the terms. His salary was far more than any other player was earning at the time, more than three times as much as the second-highest player. In fact, it was more than the president of the United States earned. In 1930, President Herbert Hoover earned $75,000. When Ruth was asked if he felt that a ballplayer should earn more than the president, Ruth famously replied, "Why not? I had a better year than he did."

After his two-year contract expired, the Yankees offered him $70,000 for the 1932 season. Ruth countered by asking for another two-year deal at $80,000 a year. The Depression was now two years old, though, and salaries were being cut everywhere. The two sides held out for two months before they finally reached an agreement. Ruth would get a one-year contract worth $75,000.

1932 SEASON: THE YANKEES ARE BACK ON TOP

In 1932, the slump was finally over. The Yankees were a great team again, strong in the infield and the outfield as well as on the mound and at bat. The team, with a 107–47 record, won the pennant by a landslide over the Philadelphia Athletics. Ruth himself was getting older—he was 37—and his play was declining somewhat, though he was still a great player. Younger players were now hitting better, and he held no notable records for the 1932 season. He hit 41 home runs, but for the first time since 1925, he did not lead the league in home runs. Jimmie Foxx of the Athletics did, with 58 homers. Injuries and illness kept Ruth out of several games, and it was uncertain if he would be able to participate in the World Series because of a condition that was attributed to his appendix, but there is doubt about the actual cause as no surgery was performed.

Ruth did play in the Series—it was the Yankees against the Chicago Cubs. Although he did not play exceptionally well, the World Series featured one of the most legendary events in Ruth's career—what is known as the "Called Shot."

Throughout the Series, there was much teasing and ribbing between the Cubs and Ruth; mostly it was playful, but at times, it went too far, with personal insults shot back and forth. Ruth's wife was reportedly spat upon during a game.

As Ruth stood at the plate in the fifth inning of Game 3 on October 1, 1932, exchanges of this sort were going on between him and the Cub players in the dugout. The first pitch was a strike, after which Ruth raised one finger in the direction of the Cubs' dugout, presumably to indicate that he still had two strikes left. After two balls, another strike was thrown. At this point, Ruth paused and pointed one finger in the direction

★ ★ ★ ★ ★

THE GREAT DEPRESSION

Beginning in late 1929 and lasting throughout the 1930s, the United States was struck by what is called the Great Depression. It was a period of extreme economic collapse, which caused rampant unemployment and homelessness. In 1929, the unemployment rate in the United States was 3.2 percent. By 1932, it had risen to a startling 25.2 percent. The Great Depression began after the stock market crash of October 1929, which left many people and businesses bankrupt. In the Great Plains, drought followed by dust storms caused further devastation to those who earned their living in the agricultural industry. President Herbert Hoover was widely criticized for failing to reform the American economy and end the Depression. The Depression exposed how unstable the economy was, and it took many years to recover. President Franklin D. Roosevelt, who defeated Hoover in the 1932 election, is credited with pulling the United States out of the Depression.

of the dugout, the pitcher, or center field—which one we will never be certain. On the next pitch, Ruth swung and hit a home run—his second of the day—with the ball landing high in the center-field stands. Later that day in a New York paper, a sportswriter wrote, "In the fifth, with the Cubs riding him unmercifully from the bench, Ruth pointed to center and punched a screaming liner to a spot where no ball had been hit before." The headline of the piece was "Ruth Calls Shot as He Puts Homer No. 2 in Side Pocket." The story spread that Ruth had pointed to center to indicate that he intended to hit the ball to that exact spot. At first Ruth denied it, but later he

☆ ☆ ☆ ☆ ☆

The Depression also took its toll on baseball, as it did on all businesses. Most players received pay cuts, and two players from each of the 16 teams lost their positions completely. People who were out of work could no longer afford the luxury of a baseball game. The Depression impacted baseball in lasting ways. Because teams were playing to smaller and smaller crowds, games were regularly broadcast on the radio for the first time during the Depression. These broadcasts provided an affordable way for people to enjoy America's pastime from their homes, listening to broadcasters announcing every play. Stadium lights were first used during the Depression, in an attempt by owners to stay afloat by making night games possible. Night games allowed spectators to attend games while being able to go to work during the day. The first All-Star Game was also played during the Depression, another attempt to draw crowds.

Lou Gehrig greeted Babe Ruth after Ruth hit a home run in Game 3 of the 1932 World Series against the Chicago Cubs. The home run was the famed "Called Shot," in which Ruth supposedly pointed to center field to indicate where he was going to hit the homer.

changed his story and claimed until his death that he had called the shot.

RUTH'S DECLINE

The 1932 World Series was Ruth's last real time on top. That one of his most storied moments of glory—the Called Shot— occurred during the Series is in that way fitting. Ruth's play began to decline after that. That he was aging became more evident during the 1933 season, which began with Ruth's getting a fairly major pay cut—his new contract offer was for $50,000 a year, still very high compared with that of other players, but a pay decrease of $25,000. Ruth was upset, telling

☆ ☆ ☆ ☆ ☆ ☆

THE NEGRO LEAGUES

During the years that Babe Ruth played baseball, the game was still a segregated sport. African Americans shared the same passion for the game and, although banned from playing in white professional leagues, they formed their own amateur and professional teams after the Civil War. The Cuban Giants, the first professional black baseball club, were founded in 1885. Over the next few decades, African-American ball clubs operated independently, without a formal league.

The first Negro League, the Negro National League, was started in 1920 and fell apart in 1931, because of Depression-era bankruptcy. In 1933, a second Negro National League was started and remained in existence until 1949. From 1920 until the 1940s, the Negro Southern League operated. Another league, the Negro American League, was begun in 1937. When the Negro National League folded in 1949, it was absorbed into the Negro American League, which stayed in operation until 1960.

Despite the incredible talent of the Negro Leagues, which included some of the best baseball players in history, baseball remained segregated in the United States until Jackie Robinson signed with the Brooklyn Dodgers in November 1945. Robinson played the 1946 season with the Dodgers' farm team in Montreal, Canada. Then, he made his major-league debut in April 1947.

Yankees owner Jacob Ruppert, "I expected a cut, but $25,000 is no cut, it's an amputation." Ruppert held firm to the offer. With the Depression still raging and Ruth's play declining, he was not prepared to offer Ruth a penny more. Ruth trained with his team in Florida but had not yet signed a contract. Ruppert gave him an ultimatum: "If Ruth does not sign by March 29, he will not be taken north with the team. Furthermore, if he does not come to terms by then, the present offer of $50,000 will be lowered." In the end, Ruth agreed to the new salary. To save face for Ruth, however, Ruppert told the press that he had agreed to raise Ruth's pay $2,000 to $52,000, so the public believed there had been a compromise.

On the field, Ruth was slowing down. His batting average for the 1933 season was .301—still good but a drop from his earlier days. He was a respectable player but was no longer an exceptional player. The team itself had also declined. There were no significant lineup changes, but the game did not come together for the team in the same way as the year before. The Yankees finished second in the American League that season, seven games behind the Washington Senators.

HOPES UNFULFILLED

Ruth was very open about his ambition to replace Joe McCarthy as manager of the Yankees. Ruth had claimed for some time that he would retire after the 1933 season, presumably to manage his team. Ed Barrow, the Yankees' general manager, was never going to give Ruth a shot, stating, "How can he possibly manage other men when he can't even manage himself?" Ruth may have had other opportunities to manage —Detroit Tigers owner Frank Navin showed an interest in hiring Ruth—but Ruth was stubbornly fixed on managing the Yankees. When he was not offered the job after 1933, he decided to sign up to play another year. Ruth's play further declined, and it was widely known that 1934 would be his last season as a Yankee and most likely as a player.

Babe Ruth was called safe after a Japanese pitcher tried to catch him off first base during an exhibition game in November 1934 in Tokyo. Ruth had played his last game for the New York Yankees and would be joining a new team for the 1935 season.

Ruth and his incredible baseball career were honored in various ways in 1934. He was selected to be part of the All-Star team for the second year in a row (1933 was the All-Star Game's first year), although this was more a credit to his career than his 1934 season. He was also selected to go on a baseball tour that brought him to Japan. Japan did not have a baseball league at the time, although the sport was very popular and Ruth himself was very well known. Still, it was clear that he was not going to be given a chance to manage the Yankees, so Ruth decided it was time to move on. "I'm through with the Yanks," he said. "I won't play with them unless I can manage. But they're sticking with McCarthy, and that lets me out."

THE BABE HEADS BACK TO BOSTON

With no manager's job available to him and no possibility that his pride would allow him to play for the Yankees another season, Babe Ruth needed a new plan. At the same time, Emil Fuchs, owner of the Boston Braves, was hoping to increase interest in his team to improve attendance and make it more profitable. He hoped that bringing Ruth back to Boston would solve a lot of his problems.

The offer Fuchs made to Ruth was essentially this: Ruth would sign on with the Braves for a flat salary. Ruth would be a player as well as an assistant to manager Bill McKechnie. His salary would be $25,000 a year, but he could more or less play when he liked—although the understanding was that he would play as often as he could. He was also named a vice president of the Braves and offered the opportunity to own stock in the team. Fuchs presented this offer in a letter. The section of the letter that no doubt most caught Ruth's eye was this: "If it was determined, after your affiliation with the club in 1935, that it was for the mutual interest of the club for you to take up active management on the field, there would be absolutely no handicap in having you so appointed." What Fuchs was saying was that perhaps, if circumstances allowed it, Ruth would be given a chance to manage. Ruth read the letter a little differently and began to tell everyone, including the press, that he would be the Braves' manager come 1936.

The Yankees agreed to let Ruth go—rather eagerly—and Ruth was eager to finally realize his dream to be a manager. At a party to mark the official signing of Ruth's contract with the Braves, Charles Adams, a vice president of the Braves franchise, was very unapologetic about his feelings about

Ruth, saying in a speech, "No one is fit to give orders until he can take them himself. Judging from Ruth's past career, we can hardly consider him of managerial caliber now. I certainly hope he will merit promotion as manager of the Braves. He has much to learn within the next few months. He must prove himself to be a good soldier if he is not that already, and he must gain the loyalty of his teammates." Ruth did not hear this as a warning or as foreshadowing of what was to come. Instead, he was excited about the new possibility of becoming a manager at last.

Retirement
and Death

Babe Ruth showed up to spring training in 1935 in a Boston Braves uniform. For the first time in 15 years, he was not there as a Yankee. He was also not in great shape, having ballooned to 245 pounds (111 kilograms). And age—he was now 40—was further slowing him down. Still, he was a media sensation. People flocked to see him, and he had to push his way through crowds of fans and reporters.

If his celebrity was not diminished, his skills as a player certainly were. Ruth was overweight and slow, both at running bases and playing in the outfield. At the plate, he did not hit a single home run during spring training. Team manager Bill McKechnie did not know where to play him, and certainly did not seem to be seeking Ruth's advice as his so-called assistant manager. To McKechnie, Ruth was no more than another player in the field—and not a very good one.

Ruth's role as vice president seemed equally meaningless. Although photos circulated of Ruth at a desk in a suit, his main function as a vice president was to attract media attention and to boost ticket sales. He signed autographs. He attended store openings and other photo opportunities. Rather than being given an opportunity to earn money on the team with stock options, Ruth was asked to invest $50,000 of his own money in the team. It seemed that most of the contract perks he had been so enthusiastic about were falling short.

THE SEASON BEGINS

After a series of exhibition games in which Ruth and the Braves as a whole played rather unimpressively, the 1935 season began. A crowd of 25,000 people attended the Braves' first game against the Giants. Ruth was responsible for each of the four runs the Braves scored, defeating the Giants 4-2. Although he had tried his hand at first base during spring training, Ruth was back again in the outfield, where he made a diving catch. The season went downhill from there. The Braves lost a series of games, and Ruth contributed very little, actually missing several games because of a bad cold and never playing a complete game. Any notions that bringing Ruth to the Braves would help save the franchise were a bust. The team continued to lose games and lose money. This made Ruth's opportunity to buy stock in the Braves as worthless as every other perk that had been afforded him when he signed with the team—who would want stock in a losing team? It was also becoming clear that McKechnie had no intention of leaving his position as manager to make way for Ruth to step into the role.

By May 12, Ruth wanted to quit. He asked Emil Fuchs, the owner of the Braves, to let him go on voluntary retirement, a status that would keep him part of the team but free him from playing in any games. The request was denied. Fuchs wanted to keep Ruth to his end of the bargain. The team was preparing to go on a multi-city road trip, and fans would expect to see Ruth play. Ruth agreed to go on the trip but swore he would quit when it was over, a statement that was repeated in the press. Fuchs replied to Ruth's statements by saying, "I'd be mighty sorry if he retired, but perhaps this trip will restore his peace of mind. He's been ill, and his eyes have been bothering him. He's been playing when he really should have been resting. However, if he does not show decided improvement on this trip, he will retire to pinch-hitting and coaching."

The Braves' road trip was a bad one. Ruth played badly, the team played badly, and a losing streak ensued. One highlight came on May 25 in Pittsburgh. Ruth hit three home runs in the game, the last one against pitcher Guy Bush, who was quoted as saying, "I never saw a ball hit so hard before or since. He was fat and old, but he still had that great swing. Even when he missed, you could hear the bat go swish. I can't remember anything about the first home run he hit off me that day. I guess it was just another homer. But I can't forget that last one. It's probably still going." Nobody had ever hit a ball over the roof at Forbes Field, but that is just what Ruth did. It was a spectacular home run.

GIVING UP BASEBALL FOR GOOD

That home run proved to be Ruth's last great moment with the Boston Braves. Ruth could hit, but he was not a fast runner or a sharp fielder—and he was proving to be more of a problem for Fuchs than an asset. Ruth was still enormously popular with fans, though, and it would not be wise for Fuchs to simply fire his celebrity player. Ruth was equally fed up with Fuchs by this time, and the situation finally came to a head over an issue that had nothing to do with baseball.

Babe Ruth joined the Boston Braves for the 1935 season as a player and assistant manager. He was also named a vice president of the team. Much of what Ruth thought he was promised, though, failed to pan out. Here, he sits in the dugout before a game against the Chicago Cubs on May 21. He would quit baseball in less than a month.

An ocean liner—the *Normandie*—was bound for New York City from Europe in June. It's hard to imagine today, but this was a huge society event. The *Normandie* was the newest, fastest, biggest ship of its day, and its arrival was to be met with great fanfare. Ruth and his wife were invited to a party celebrating the arrival, and he wanted more than anything to be there. Fuchs would not release him from a scheduled game. That was the last straw for Ruth. On June 2, he told reporters that he was done with baseball. Fuchs responded by saying, "I have given Ruth his unconditional release, and he is through with the Braves in every way." Babe Ruth was officially retired.

COULD RUTH HAVE MANAGED?

That baseball never gave Babe Ruth a chance to manage was devastating to him. For all the speculation that he could never handle the job, there was very little to support claims that he would fail. Although he had been a rebellious player throughout his career, often pushing back when given direction he did not agree with, he was a smart player who lived baseball. Of what it takes to manage well, Ruth wrote in his book, *Babe Ruth's Own Book of Baseball*, "A real manager takes advantage of every little thing to help his team. Fellows like [New York Giants manager John] McGraw and [Yankees manager Miller] Huggins eat and sleep and drink baseball. It's their very life—and the years give them a knowledge that can't be beat." Ruth could have been describing himself. In the same book, he talks about the differences between players who have gone to college and those who have not, and seems to be addressing one cause of his own stubbornness as a player:

> Some people argue that college men are better ballplayers than the others. I don't believe that. But I do believe that the boy who has gone through college is quicker to learn inside baseball. He's more willing to learn, too. The sandlotter, a

lot of times, is a stubborn cuss who doesn't like instruction. The average college fellow realizes that he doesn't know it all and is willing to take advice from the players who have been around longer than he has.

For years after her husband's death, Claire Ruth remained angry at baseball for its refusal to offer Ruth a manager's job. Babe Ruth biographer Robert W. Creamer argues in his book, *Babe: The Legend Comes to Life*, that Ruth certainly could have managed. Creamer wrote that Ed Barrow's comments about Ruth—"How can he manage other men when he can't even manage himself?"—spread like wildfire through the baseball world and were repeated time and time again until it became what Creamer called "cliché, a petrified truth." Creamer added that "other people repeated it profoundly as though they had just made it up." Whether Ruth would have made a good manager is impossible to answer because he never got the opportunity.

LIFE AFTER BASEBALL

On June 3, the day after he retired, Babe and Claire Ruth drove to New York. Claire would later claim that Babe cried the entire way. He had no job offers other than one from a minor-league team in Florida. Ruth would never get a chance to manage a baseball team. He still attended baseball games, however. The National League gave him a lifetime free pass to all of its games. The American League did no such thing, and Ruth had to pay to attend Yankee games.

He played golf, bowled, had some car accidents, and drank. He fished and hunted. In the media, sightings of Ruth were generally reported as sad events. His retirement came with bitterness and resentment rather than dignity and mutual respect between himself and baseball, although he was one of the first five players inducted into the Baseball Hall of Fame in 1936.

Babe Ruth's dream after playing baseball was to be a manager. The closest he ever got was in 1938 when the Brooklyn Dodgers hired him as a first-base coach. He stayed with the job for one season.

The media were not so kind to him right after his retirement. He was often depicted as having fallen from fame and glory to a pathetic sort of irrelevance. The Associated Press had this to say of seeing Babe Ruth at the first game of the 1936 World Series:

> George Herman Ruth has finally faded into legend. He was the most forlorn figure in the Polo Grounds today, snapped now and then by a photographer who noticed him in a box down the first-base line near Mayor [Fiorello] LaGuardia and Jimmy Walker.
>
> But there was none of the fanfare that attended him at the Series last year. He sat with his wife and daughter and Kate Smith, the singer. And when the urchins came round for signatures, most of them wanted Kate's.

Ruth did not help paint any better picture. When interviewed, he often turned melancholy, making statements such as, "I wanted to stay in baseball more than I ever wanted anything in my life, but in 1935, there was no job for me, and that embittered me." His marriage reportedly faltered as well. His daughter Dorothy published a book in 1988 called *My Dad, the Babe*, in which she was very open about her feelings for her stepmother. "Not only were her mental capacities for anything but baseball statistics and money slipping," she wrote, "but her lush beauty was also rapidly deteriorating. My father and Claire had only been married for seven years, but she looked as though twenty horrendous years had passed."

In 1938, Ruth got the closest thing he would ever get to a manager's job when Brooklyn Dodgers general manager Larry MacPhail asked him to join the team as a first-base coach. Ruth perhaps hoped this would lead to his becoming a manager, but after one season it was clear that it would never happen. Ruth quit after one season and never held another job in professional baseball.

FAILING HEALTH

By the end of the 1930s, Ruth weighed about 270 pounds (122 kilograms). While playing golf in 1939, Ruth had what went undiagnosed but was probably a heart attack. Another one followed the next year. He was offered a film role—playing himself in *Pride of the Yankees*, the story of Lou Gehrig—in 1942, and the part required him to lose about 40 pounds (18 kilograms), which he did. During filming, though, he caught a bad cold that led to pneumonia. He kept active during World War II, but after the war ended, he began to have more medical problems. He started to experience pain over his left eye. He thought it was just a sinus infection, but he actually had a cancerous growth on the left side of his neck. He was kept at French Hospital in Manhattan for three months to get

★ ★ ★ ★ ★ ★

RUTH'S WARTIME ACTIVITIES

Babe Ruth was known for his generosity, and during World War II, he did his part in several ways. He spent $100,000 on war bonds, which were sold to help fund the war effort, and he also served as a spokesman to encourage others to invest in war bonds. Ruth volunteered for the Red Cross and organized three charity golf matches against his former baseball rival Ty Cobb. He lost the first match, won the second, and lost the third.

In August 1942, Ruth participated in a charity game at Yankee Stadium—his first return there since 1934, and in 1943 he coached a team of servicemen in another benefit game held at Yankee Stadium. Ruth also participated in bowling matches to raise money for the war effort, and he made visits to veterans' hospitals.

treatment. He lost 80 pounds (36 kilograms). In March 1947, new baseball commissioner A. B. Chandler declared Sunday, April 27, Babe Ruth Day, and ceremonies honoring the player would be held in stadiums across the country. The biggest celebration would be in New York City, and Ruth himself would attend.

Babe Ruth showed up at Yankee Stadium, where 60,000 people gathered to honor him. He was very thin, and his voice was weak. He spoke to the crowd, saying, "The only real game in the world, I think, is baseball." He ended his speech saying, "There's been so many lovely things said about me, I'm glad I had the chance to thank everybody. Thank you." He waved and returned to the dugout.

DECLINE AND DEATH

Ruth appeared at Yankee Stadium again in June 1948, this time to celebrate the twenty-fifth anniversary of the ballpark. His health had further declined, and he appeared weaker than ever. He wore his Yankee uniform, which hung off his tiny frame. Before leaving the stadium that day, he said to former teammate Joe Dugan, "Joe, I'm gone. I'm gone, Joe." Both men cried.

Soon after, Ruth returned to the hospital, where he received hundreds of letters of support from fans and a phone call from President Harry Truman. He answered every letter. He continued to be able to walk and talk, and he attended the premiere of a film about his life, *The Babe Ruth Story*, although he left before the film ended because he felt too ill. He returned to the hospital for the last time. The cancer continued to eat away at his body. He lost more and more weight and could barely speak. He died on August 16, 1948, at the age of 53.

For two days, Ruth's body lay in Yankee Stadium, where more than 200,000 people came to pay respects. His funeral at St. Patrick's Cathedral was attended by 9,500 mourners, with tens of thousands more on the streets outside. He is buried at

Wearing his No. 3 uniform, Babe Ruth received a standing ovation on June 13, 1948, at Yankee Stadium. He was attending ceremonies to mark the twenty-fifth anniversary of the opening of Yankee Stadium. The Yankees also retired Ruth's number that day.

the Gate of Heaven Cemetery in Hawthorne, New York, where his tombstone reads, "May The Divine Spirit That Animated Babe Ruth To Win The Crucial Game Of Life Inspire The Youth Of America." His wife, Claire, was buried next to him upon her death in 1976.

His daughter from his first marriage, Dorothy, died in 1989. A year earlier, she wrote a book, *My Dad, the Babe*. Dorothy grew up believing that Helen Ruth was her natural mother and did not learn the identity of her birth mother, Juanita Jennings, until she was 59 years old. Jennings was a family friend whom Dorothy had grown up knowing and loving. Babe Ruth's second daughter, Julia, also wrote a book about her famous father, *Major League Dad: A Daughter's Cherished Memories*.

RUTH'S LEGACY

Babe Ruth was one of the most talented and well-loved baseball players of all time. His mark of 714 career home runs was the major-league record for 39 years. Even beyond the impressive statistics, his impact was huge. He is frequently credited with saving baseball after the so-called Black Sox scandal, in which players on the Chicago White Sox agreed to intentionally lose the 1919 World Series for money. The scandal turned off many fans, and many say it was Babe Ruth's big personality and lovable character that allowed baseball to recover. He affected the game in other ways. His high salaries had the effect of raising pay for all baseball players. He was a cultural icon. During World War II, it is said that when American soldiers shouted insults about the Japanese emperor, the Japanese came back with insults directed at Ruth. In 1925, Babe Ruth and Charlie Chaplin were named the most widely known celebrities in the United States. Ruth continues to be one of the most celebrated players and personalities in baseball history. As journalist Tom Meany put it, "Few celebrities, ballplayers or crooners, actors or politicians, achieve a grip on the public which extends beyond their active and productive years."

REMEMBERING BABE RUTH

Babe Ruth was one of those rare athletes who, when you saw him play—whether you like sports or follow teams or understand all the nuances of a given game—made you realize that you were watching a genius, a legend. You know it is something to tell your grandchildren. Everyone who ever saw Babe Ruth swing a bat or just greet a crowd was forever moved by the experience. In fact, a man reportedly died from "excitement" while watching Babe Ruth at bat in 1920. On February 6, 1995—100 years after Babe Ruth's birth—the *Sporting News* ran a special 100-year anniversary edition in which letters from people sharing their Babe Ruth memories were printed. Here are some examples of the ways in which Babe Ruth touched the lives of those who saw him play.

☆ ☆ ☆ ☆ ☆

I first saw the Babe at the 1939 New York World's Fair. Then retired, he came out on a Saturday morning and hit fungoes to us kids. I never forgot it. Of all the sports legends, the Babe stands above the rest.

George Herman Ruth is known by all, regardless of age or walk of life. Pictures of his stance and swing and stories of his big heart, enthusiasm and lifestyle will never be forgotten.

The Babe represents the spirit of the game and an era when it was played for the love of the game and not for the greed that is threatening to ruin a national tradition.

—Bill Cassard, Newnan, Georgia

☆ ☆ ☆ ☆ ☆

Some of my earliest recollections are of tales of Ruth from my father. The Yankees had spring training in New Orleans from 1922–24, and my father had the opportunity to see them (and Ruth) in person. Babe was larger than life, and my father became a dyed-in-the-wool Yankee fan for the rest of his life.

In turn, my brother and I picked up the zeal and remain today ardent baseball and Yankee fans. For that I am truly grateful to my father. He gave me many things, but none that created a common ground like baseball and the Yankees. On February 6, I will remember Babe's birth and celebrate the life my brother and I shared with my Dad.

Thank you for asking about this great man.

—Albert Cyrus, New Orleans

☆ ☆ ☆ ☆ ☆

It was my good fortune to see Babe Ruth play three times. Babe Ruth was baseball when I was a kid. In 192[5], my father took me and my older brother to New York to see the Bambino play. Ruth had just resumed his place in the lineup after being sidelined with his historic "bellyache." The Yankees beat the Washington Senators that day, but Lou Gehrig upstaged the Babe by hitting two homers while the Bambino managed only a single.

In 1931 or '32, my aunt and uncle invited me to go to Washington with them to see the Yankees play. This time I was not disappointed. "General" Alvin Crowder of the Senators had a shutout going into the ninth inning. The Babe stepped to the plate with a runner on first and blasted a home run off the top of the right-field scoreboard. What a thrill. After the game, my uncle asked if I wanted to wait to see if I could get autographs of some of the players. I waited patiently under the stands as player after player came out, but no Babe. Other kids suggested that he usually took a nap after each game to avoid the crowd. Another said he had heard that there was a special tunnel that led from the dressing room to the Babe's waiting car. After most of the

The mystique and legend of Babe Ruth lives on to this day. Here, his grave is shown on October 28, 2004, decorated by fans of the New York Yankees and the Boston Red Sox. The Red Sox had just won the 2004 World Series, ending the "Curse of the Bambino," which said that the Sox would never win a championship after selling Ruth to the Yankees.

autograph hunters had left, Gehrig approached. I asked if he would sign my score card. His reply was, "Not today, Sonny." Dejectedly, I trudged back to the car and related my story to my aunt and uncle. Two weeks later I received a plain white envelope postmarked New York. Opening it I found a white index card with the signature "Babe Ruth" in the center in black ink. My aunt had written the Babe in care of the Yankees and told him of her nephew's disappointment in not seeing him after the game. I treasure that autograph today.

The third time I saw the Babe play was in 1935 when he was with the Boston Braves. The team was headed north from spring training and stopped in Fayetteville, N.C., for an exhibition game with the North Carolina State team. Babe played five innings at first base and went hitless. The next day's local paper ran a headline, "Lefty Freeman strikes out Babe Ruth." It did not mention the score, but the big leaguers won with ease. Within a few months, my boyhood idol would be out of baseball.

—Edgar Wyatt, Raleigh, North Carolina

☆ ☆ ☆ ☆ ☆

Born in 1935, I was too young to see Babe Ruth play. My Dad used to tell me stories about him and of seeing him play at Navin Field in Detroit.

I don't remember the year my Dad and I went to Briggs Stadium to see the Babe in his farewell to the public. I was surprised to see how frail he looked. He had on a cashmere topcoat and stooped over.

As the Babe tried to talk into the microphone, I noticed tears running down my Dad's cheeks. (Naturally, I started crying.) I could not make out most of his words because of his hoarse voice, but I did not miss his "Thank you!" As the 50-plus thousands cheered and stomped their feet, my Dad had to take his glasses off because of tears. After what seemed like 15 minutes, I started to cry, too.

The way he stood there and tried to talk made my Dad a total mess. It was a day I will always remember and see as clearly as today.

The Babe and my Dad showed me something I will never forget.

—Jim Penfield, Port Richey, Florida

STATISTICS

BABE RUTH
Primary position: Center field (also P)

Full name: George Herman Ruth
Born: February 6, 1895, Baltimore,
Maryland • Died: August 16, 1948,
New York, New York • Height: 6'2" •
Weight: 215 lbs. • Teams: Boston Red
Sox (1914–1919), New York Yankees
(1920–1934), Boston Braves (1935)

★ ★ ★ ★ ★

YEAR	TEAM	G	AB	H	HR	RBI	BA
1914	BOS	5	10	2	0	2	.200
1915	BOS	42	92	29	4	21	.315
1916	BOS	67	136	37	3	15	.272
1917	BOS	52	123	40	2	12	.325
1918	BOS	95	317	95	11	66	.300
1919	BOS	130	432	139	29	114	.322
1920	NYY	142	458	172	54	137	.376
1921	NYY	152	540	204	59	171	.378
1922	NYY	110	406	128	35	99	.315
1923	NYY	152	522	205	41	131	.393
1924	NYY	153	529	200	46	121	.378
1925	NYY	98	359	104	25	66	.290
1926	NYY	152	495	184	47	146	.372
1927	NYY	151	540	192	60	.164	.356

Key: BOS = Boston Red Sox; NYY = New York Yankees; BSN = Boston Braves;
G = Games; AB = At-bats; H = Hits; HR = Home runs; RBI = Runs batted in;
BA = Batting average; W = Wins; L = Losses; ERA = Earned run average;
SO = Strikeouts; BB = Bases on balls

YEAR	TEAM	G	AB	H	HR	RBI	BA
1928	NYY	154	536	173	54	142	.323
1929	NYY	135	499	172	46	154	.345
1930	NYY	145	518	186	49	153	.359
1931	NYY	145	534	199	46	163	.373
1932	NYY	133	457	156	41	137	.341
1933	NYY	137	459	138	34	103	.301
1934	NYY	125	365	105	22	84	.288
1935	BSN	28	72	13	6	12	.181
TOTALS		2,503	8,399	2,873	714	2,213	.342

PITCHING

YEAR	TEAM	G	W–L	ERA	SO	BB
1914	BOS	4	2–1	3.91	3	7
1915	BOS	32	18–8	2.44	112	85
1916	BOS	44	23–12	1.75	170	118
1917	BOS	41	24–13	2.01	128	108
1918	BOS	20	13–7	2.22	40	49
1919	BOS	17	9–5	2.97	30	58
1920	NYY	1	1–0	4.50	0	2
1921	NYY	2	2–0	9.00	2	9
1930	NYY	1	1–0	3.00	3	2
1933	NYY	1	1–0	5.00	0	3
TOTALS		163	94–46	2.28	488	441

Key: BOS = Boston Red Sox; NYY = New York Yankees; BSN = Boston Braves;
G = Games; AB = At-bats; H = Hits; HR = Home runs; RBI = Runs batted in;
BA = Batting average; W = Wins; L = Losses; ERA = Earned run average;
SO = Strikeouts; BB = Bases on balls

CHRONOLOGY

1895   **February 6**   Born George Herman Ruth in Baltimore to Kate and George Ruth, Sr.

1902   His father takes him to St. Mary's Industrial School for Boys, where George is enrolled as a student.

1914   **February 27**   Leaves St. Mary's to play professional baseball with the Baltimore Orioles, a minor-league team. With the Orioles, he picks up the nickname "Babe."

         July 9   Sold to his first major-league team, the Boston Red Sox.

         October 17   Marries Helen Woodford.

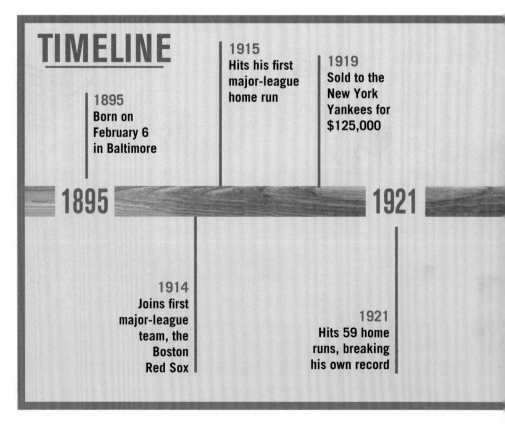

TIMELINE

1895 Born on February 6 in Baltimore

1915 Hits his first major-league home run

1919 Sold to the New York Yankees for $125,000

1895 — **1921**

1914 Joins first major-league team, the Boston Red Sox

1921 Hits 59 home runs, breaking his own record

1915   **May 6** Hits his first major-league home run.

1916   The Red Sox win the World Series for the second year in a row. Babe Ruth pitches in the second game, a 14-inning contest that the Red Sox win 2-1.

1919   Sets a major-league record for home runs, with 29.

       December 26 Sold to the New York Yankees for $125,000.

1920   **September 20** Hits his 100th career home run.

1921   Ends the season with 59 home runs, a new record; the Yankees take the American League pennant.

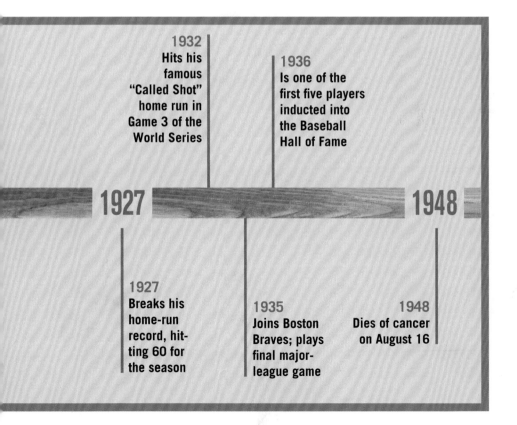

1932
Hits his famous "Called Shot" home run in Game 3 of the World Series

1936
Is one of the first five players inducted into the Baseball Hall of Fame

1927

1948

1927
Breaks his home-run record, hitting 60 for the season

1935
Joins Boston Braves; plays final major-league game

1948
Dies of cancer on August 16

1922   Suspended from play for the first six weeks
        of the season for participating in a barnstorming
        tour.

1923   **April 18** Yankee Stadium opens; Babe Ruth hits a
        home run during this debut game against the Boston
        Red Sox.

        May 12 Hits his 200th career home run.

1924   Wins the American League batting title with a
        .378 average.

1925   **September 8** Hits his 300th career home run.

1927   **September 2** Hits his 400th career home run.

        September 30 Hits his 60th home run of the season,
        setting a new major-league record.

1928   **October 9** Hits three home runs in a World Series
        game for the second time in his career.

1929   **January 11** Helen Ruth dies in a house fire.

        April 17 Marries Claire Hodgson.

        August 11 Hits his 500th career home run.

1932   **October 1** Hits his famous "Called Shot" home run
        in Game 3 of the World Series.

1934   **September 29** Hits his 708th home run as a Yankee.

1935   **February 2** Quits the Yankees and signs up with the
        Boston Braves.

        June 2 Quits professional baseball.

1936   Is among the first five players inducted into the
        Baseball Hall of Fame.

1938   **June 18** Joins the Brooklyn Dodgers as a first-
        base coach.

1947   April 27 Attends Babe Ruth Day at Yankee Stadium.

1948   August 16 Dies of cancer in New York

1949   April 19 A monument to Babe Ruth is erected at Yankee Stadium.

GLOSSARY

American League   One of the two leagues that are a part of Major League Baseball in the United States. The American League was established in 1900 and became a major league a year later.

at-bat   An official turn at batting that is charged to a baseball player, except when the player walks, sacrifices, is hit by a pitched ball, or is interfered with by a catcher. At-bats are used to calculate a player's batting average and slugging percentage.

ball   A pitch that does not pass over home plate in the strike zone. A batter who receives four balls gets a walk.

baseball commissioner   The highest-ranking office in Major League Baseball.

batter's box   The area to the left and right of home plate in which the batter must be standing for fair play to take place.

batting average   The number of hits a batter gets divided by the number of times the player is at bat. For example, 3 hits in 10 at-bats would be a .300 batting average.

bunt   A ball hit softly so that it rolls to a particular spot in the infield. A bunt is usually hit by holding the bat loosely and letting the ball bounce off it rather than swinging the bat.

catcher   The player who crouches behind home plate and signals to the pitcher what type of pitch to throw. This player also catches the pitches the batter misses or does not swing at as well as covers home plate during defensive plays.

cleanup hitter   The fourth batter in the lineup, usually a power hitter. The team hopes runners are on base for the "cleanup" hitter to drive home. Ideally, the first three batters of the game would get on base, so that the fourth batter could "clean up" the bases with a grand slam.

contract   A binding written agreement. In baseball, a player signs a contract that establishes his salary for a set number of years to play for a particular team.

curveball   A pitch that curves on its way to the plate, thanks to the spin a pitcher places on the ball when throwing. Also known as a "breaking ball."

Dead Ball Era   A period in baseball from roughly 1900 to 1920 in which games were not high-scoring and the focus was more on fielding strategy that hitting home runs. The main batting strategy was to score runs through walks, base hits, bunts, and stolen bases.

double   A hit that gets the batter to second base without the aid of a fielding error.

doubleheader   Two baseball games played by the same teams on the same day.

dugout   A structure in which players sit during game time while not playing on the field.

earned run average   The number of earned runs that a pitcher allows every nine innings. It is computed by multiplying the total number of earned runs by nine and dividing by the number of innings pitched.

error   When a defensive player makes a mistake that results in a runner reaching base or advancing a base, an error is designated by the game's scorer.

exhibition game   A game that does not count in the season's final standings.

fungo   A ball that is tossed in the air by the batter and is hit on its way down.

Green Monster   The left-field wall at Boston's Fenway Park, nicknamed after its color and height—37 feet (11 meters).

grounder   A ball that is hit and hops or rolls on the ground.

hit and run   A play in which base runners begin to run before the ball is hit and the batter tries to make contact with the pitch.

home plate   A five-sided rubber "plate" at which the batter stands to hit and which a base runner has to cross to score a run.

home run   When a batter hits a ball into the stands in fair territory, it is a home run. The batter may also hit an inside-the-park home run if the ball never leaves the playing field and the runner is able to reach home plate without stopping before being tagged by a defensive player. A home run counts as one run, and if there are any runners on base when a home run is hit, they too score.

line drive   A batted ball, usually hit hard, that never gets too far off the ground. Typically a line drive will get beyond the infield without touching the ground, or will be hit directly at a player and be caught before it touches the ground.

lineup   A list that is presented to the umpire and opposing coach before the start of the game that contains the order in which the batters will bat as well as the defensive fielding positions they will play.

Live Ball Era   The period in baseball after 1920 in which scores of games were significantly higher as teams began to focus their strategy on offense with powerful batters.

major league   Either of the two primary U.S. professional baseball leagues, the American League and the National League.

minor league   Any professional league other than the major league.

National League   One of the two leagues that are a part of Major League Baseball in the United States. The National League was established in 1876.

Negro Leagues   The leagues that were made up of professional baseball teams with African-American players. The leagues formed in the years in which baseball was segregated in the United States.

pennant   The title in the American League and National League. In Babe Ruth's day, the pennant went to the first-place team in each league. Today, each league has two rounds of play-offs, with the champion earning the pennant. The two pennant winners meet in the World Series.

pinch-hit   To substitute for another teammate at bat.

runs batted in (RBI)   The number of runs that score as a direct result of a batter's hit(s) are the runs batted in by that batter. The major-league record is 191 RBIs for a single year by one batter.

rookie   A player who is playing his first season on a professional team.

rotation   The series of pitchers on a baseball team who regularly start successive games in turn.

scout   A person who seeks undiscovered talent, such as a baseball player, to sign to a professional contract.

single   A hit that gets the batter to first base without the aid of a fielding error.

slump   A period of poor or losing play by a team or an individual player.

spring training   A period of practice and exhibition games in professional baseball that begins in late winter and goes until the start of the season in spring.

stolen base   When a runner successfully advances to the next base while the pitcher is delivering a pitch.

strike   A pitch that is swung at and missed or a pitch that is in the strike zone and is not swung at. Three strikes and the batter is out.

strike zone   The area directly over home plate up to the batter's chest (roughly where the batter's uniform lettering is) and down to his or her knees. Different umpires have slightly different strike zones, and players only ask that they be consistent.

sweep   To win every game in a tournament or series.

triple   A hit that gets the batter to third base without the aid of a fielding error.

umpire   The official who rules on plays. For most baseball games, a home-plate umpire calls balls and strikes, and other umpires in the infield rule on outs at bases.

walk   When a batter gets four balls and fewer than three strikes and advances to first base.

BIBLIOGRAPHY

Creamer, Robert W. *Babe: The Legend Comes to Life.* New York: Fireside, 1974.

Montville, Leigh. *The Big Bam: The Life and Times of Babe Ruth.* New York: Doubleday, 2006.

Ruth, George Herman. *Babe Ruth's Own Book of Baseball.* New York: G.P. Putnam's Sons, 1928.

Shaughnessy, Dan. *The Curse of the Bambino.* New York: Penguin Books, 1990.

Sobol, Ken. *Babe Ruth and the American Dream.* New York: Random House, 1974.

Tygiel, Jules. *Past Time: Baseball as History.* New York: Oxford University Press, 2000.

FURTHER READING

Aron, Paul. *Did Babe Ruth Call His Shot? And Other Unsolved Mysteries of Baseball.* Hoboken, New Jersey: John Wiley & Sons Inc., 2005.

Beim, George, with Julia Ruth Stevens. *Babe Ruth: A Daughter's Portrait.* Dallas, Texas: Taylor Publishing Company, 1998.

Brother Gilbert. *Young Babe Ruth: His Early Life and Baseball Career, from the Memoirs of a Xaverian Brother.* Jefferson, North Carolina: McFarland & Company, 1999.

Gutman, Bill. *It's Outta Here! The History of the Home Run from Babe Ruth to Barry Bonds.* Dallas, Texas: Taylor Publishing Company, 2005.

Jenkinson, Bill. *The Year Babe Ruth Hit 104 Home Runs: Recrowning Baseball's Greatest Slugger.* New York: Carroll & Graf, 2007.

Shaughnessy, Dan. *Reversing the Curse: Inside the 2004 Boston Red Sox.* Boston: Houghton Mifflin, 2005.

Stout, Glenn. *Yankees Century: 100 Years of New York Yankees Baseball.* Boston: Houghton Mifflin, 2002.

Trachtenberg, Leo. *The Wonder Team: The True Story of the Incomparable 1927 New York Yankees.* Bowling Green, Ohio: Bowling Green University Popular Press, 1995.

WEB SITES

BabeRuth.com: The Official Web Site of the Sultan of Swat
http://www.baberuth.com/

Babe Ruth Birthplace and Museum
http://www.baberuthmuseum.com/

Babe Ruth Central: The Site That Ruth Built
http://www.baberuthcentral.com

The Babe Ruth Times

http://xroads.virginia.edu/~UG02/yeung/Baberuth/home.html

Baseball Almanac

http://www.baseball-almanac.com

Baseball Reference

http://www.baseball-reference.com

The National Baseball Hall of Fame and Museum

http://baseballhalloffame.org/

The Official Site of Major League Baseball

http://mlb.mlb.com

PICTURE CREDITS

INDEX

Adams, Charles, 84–85
African Americans, 81
All-Star Games
    first, 79, 83
American League, 22, 28, 34,
    54, 58, 70, 82, 91
    founded, 2
    pennants, 59, 68, 73, 75, 77
    teams, 2, 23

Babe: The Legend Comes to Life
    (Creamer), 41, 63, 91
*Babe Ruth and the American
    Dream* (Sobol), 43
*Babe Ruth's Own Book of Base-
    ball*
    childhood in, 3–4
    major leagues in, 27–28, 44,
        71–73
    managers in, 90–91
Babe Ruth Story, The
    childhood in, 4
    contracts in, 13
    early baseball in, 19–20
Babe Ruth Story, The (movie),
    95
Baker, Newton, 49
Baltimore, Maryland
    Babe Ruth Museum in, 63
    childhood in, 2–4, 5, 7–11,
        14, 20, 73
    family in, 5, 14
Baltimore Orioles (minor
    league)
    coaches, 15, 19
    contract with, 13, 25
    exhibition games, 17, 21–23,
        25
    management and ownership,
        10–11, 15, 19, 20, 21, 25–26
    scouts, 10
    spring training, 14–17, 19–20
    teammates, 14–17, 19, 23, 25
Baltimore Terrapins, 21, 25

Barnstorming tours, 61, 68, 83
Barrow, Edward
    and the Boston Red Sox,
        48–50
    Yankees' general manager,
        82, 91
Barry, Jack
    and the Boston Red Sox, 48
Baseball
    commission, 25–26
    commissioner, 95
    fans, 2, 7, 21, 32, 57–58, 60–
        61, 63, 66, 74, 86, 88, 97, 99
    history, 1, 21, 40–41, 59
    pre-Ruth era, 2, 40–41, 59, 97
    rules, 1
Batting averages, 45
    first season, 36
    major league, 57–59, 67–68,
        70, 82
    titles, 68
Bedient, Hugh, 33
"Betsy Bingle," 67
Big Bam, The (Montville)
    baseball in, 19–20, 45
    early years in, 5, 7–8
Black Sox scandal, 97
Boston Braves
    contract, 84, 87
    fans, 86, 88
    management, 84–85, 86–88,
        90
    spring training, 86–87
Boston Red Sox, 11
    1915 season, 38–42
    1916 season, 44–45
    exhibition games, 38
    fans, 57
    games against, 66
    management and ownership,
        27–28, 32–34, 39, 43, 45,
        47–50, 52–53, 55–56
    minor-league team, 33–34,
        36

ABOUT THE AUTHOR

TRACY BROWN COLLINS received her master's degree in European cultural history from the University of Amsterdam and has more than 12 years' experience in the publishing industry. She has written and edited several nonfiction books for young adults, as well as teacher and student guides for various educational publishers. She lives with her husband and dogs in the Netherlands.